Para
Monica
De
Patty xxx.

Persian Cats

The Complete Owners Guide from
Kitten to Old Age

Buying, Caring for, Grooming, Health,
Training and Understanding Your
Persian Cat or Kitten

By Rosemary Kendall

Copyright and Trademarks

Disclaimer and Legal Notice

Foreword

For the past 50 years, I've had cats of some kind in my life. As a young woman, I kept company with a motley assortment of "alley cats," all strays, which I rescued. My parents were unbelievably tolerant of their young "crazy cat lady" in training.

As I struck out on my own, I started to learn more about distinct breeds, going through relationships with a lovely Somali, a somewhat ill-tempered Himalayan, and two fantastic Russian Blue mixes.

I've known a sturdy and well-mannered British Shorthair, a thoroughly intelligent, albeit demanding Siamese, and an exotic and beguiling Savannah cat.

None of the cats in my life were ever long-haired. I said I didn't want the mess, complained that I didn't have time for the grooming, and declared that I didn't like the look. Then, at a vet clinic, one of the techs handed me a Smoke Persian kitten.

I've always had something of a weakness for blue cats, and looking into his round, sweet eyes centered in a charmingly flat face, my heart melted. "He needs a home," she said, smiling triumphantly because it was clear that the instant "he" passed into my hands, the kitten had a home.

Ashe wasn't pedigreed in the sense that he came with papers, but as I began to learn more about Persians, I knew he was a quality animal that had, for reasons I could never fathom, been abandoned as a baby.

He grew into a sturdy and placid fellow, the undisputed and regal lord of the manor. Most of the time Ashe draped himself elegantly against a well-chosen background, but at other moments he was playful and kittenish well into old age.

Since he wasn't pedigreed, and not wanting to bring even more cats into my life, I had him neutered. Many times since, I've wished I hadn't. His disposition was so superb, I would have liked to have seen those genes passed on.

As it happens, however, Ashe got me hooked on Persians, and within five years I was running my own cattery. This was a most unexpected development in my life, and a vocation and avocation that has consumed me for many years.

I hope to give you an introduction to Persians and to their basic care, as well as some insight into life with cats in general.

I'd like to tell you that I'm a purist, but the truth is that I'm a dyed-in-the-wool ailurophile, a cat lover. If it purrs and says "meow," I'm pretty much hooked.

So, allow me to introduce to you what some sources say is the most popular of all companion cats, the Persian.

Acknowledgments

In writing this book, I also sought tips, advice, photos, and opinions from many experts of the Persian breed.

In particular I wish to thank the following wonderful experts for going out of their way to help and contribute:

Jenny Nicholas of Gemkin Persians (see bonus chapter 1)
www.gemkinpersians.com

Amber Lea Morgan of Rarebreed Cattery (bonus chapter 2)
www.rarebreedcattery.com

Joan Donahue-Ulmer of KaristaKats Himalayans
www.karistakats.com

Shannon McGraw of Meow House
www.meowhousekittens.com

Molly Barr of Mythicbells Persians
www.mythicbells.com

Carole Gainsbury of Caszan Persians
www.caszan.co.uk

Pat Gallagher of Cleokat Persians
www.cleokat.com

For further details of all of the above — see chapter 4/5.

Table of Contents

Table of Contents

Table of Contents

Table of Contents

Table of Contents

Table of Contents

Table of Contents

Chapter 1 - The World of the Persian Cat

The Persian is the most popular of all cat breeds in North America and enjoys a similar degree of favor in Great Britain and the rest of Europe. They are one of the most readily recognized of all companion breeds and are available in a wide variety of colors and patterns.

What is a "Registered" Pedigree?

Before we go on to talk specifically about the Persian, let me clear up any confusion about what it means for a cat to have a registered pedigree.

Catteries list themselves with one or more of the major cat registries as further proof of the legitimacy of their bloodlines and the authenticity of their breed claims.

There are a number of cat registries, but the largest are the Cat Fanciers' Association (CFA) and The International Cat Association (TICA).

If a pedigreed cat is to be exhibited in a show organized by either group, the animal must be registered with that group.

Not all kittens born to such catteries are show quality, however, so "pet quality" kittens are made available to potential buyers. While this is not the only way to acquire a Persian cat, animals with registered pedigrees are still the finest examples of the breed you can find.

Brief History of the Persian Breed

The Persian breed as it is known today is the result of more than 150 years of careful work by loving enthusiasts to cultivate a companion animal that is both beautiful and personable.

Like most cat breeds, it's difficult to exactly pin down the origin of the Persian, but there are many records of diplomats returning to Europe in the 1800s with long-haired cats from various Eastern countries.

Most of these cats were named according to their country of origin, hence, Persians from Persia (Iran). However, there are also records of long-haired cats that were brought back to Europe in the 1300s with the Crusaders, and references to similar cats in Italy in the 1600s, especially those owned by the renowned traveler Pietro della Valle. In "Voyages de

Pietro della Valle," the author talks of gray cats with glossy, long fur that were found in the Khorazan province of Persia, saying they were brought from India by Portuguese sailors.

Since the dominant street cat in Europe was the European Shorthair, an ancestor of the burly British Shorthair of today, these exotic cats with their long, flowing coats were instantly sought after.

Many became the pampered pets of royalty, appearing at the court of France and in Buckingham Palace. Two blue Persians kept company with Queen Victoria of England.

It was in England, in fact, that cat fanciers began purposeful breeding programs to cultivate the Persian into a refined and highly popular breed. The first Persians were prominently exhibited at the first modern cat show in 1871, held at the Crystal Palace in London.

Since the 1800s, breeders have worked to incorporate the most prized physical traits into the Persian gene pool including round heads with small ears and short noses, large eyes, cobby bodies, and heavy boning.

Persians were imported to the United States at the beginning of the 20th century, with the blue and silver colorations proving especially popular. As more color variations were developed, the Persian became the most loved of all companion breeds, not only for its handsome appearance, but also for its adaptable and agreeable nature.

Adoption Considerations

Before adopting an animal of any breed, it's important to understand as much as you can about their physical needs, personality, and overall care requirements — which is why you're reading this book!

I'll give you a brief overview of the major factors to consider here in the first chapter, and then go into greater detail in subsequent chapters.

Physical Characteristics

Although heavily boned, Persians are medium-sized cats when compared to the true feline giants like the Maine

Coon. Most Persians fall into a weight range of 7-12 pounds / 3.17-5.44 kg.

The coat is long and thick, falling elegantly over a cobby body and forming a ruff at the neck. The short, straight tail is heavily plumed. The texture of the hair is silky and when well-groomed, smooth and dense, often feeling like rich velvet.

Large round eyes flank a flat, small nose and the ears are very small and round, generally with generous hair at the base. Typically, the ears tilt forward, but may also have some tendency to lie flatter against the head.

There are different facial types recognized for the breed including:

- *Traditional or Doll Face Persians* have a shortened nose, but there is still a clear muzzle present.

- *Peke-Face or Ultra-Typed Persians* result from a mutation and have overly accentuated, flattened facial features.

The legs are short, and it is not unusual for the belly hair to touch the ground, which is why most owners have their Persian's "undercarriage" shaved or cut back on a regular basis.

Persians can throw large litters of kittens, with as many as 14 possible. On average, however, the number of babies will be 3-5, all looking like adorable little powder puffs.

Originally, Persians were somewhat similar to long-haired Angoras, but with selective breeding, the Persian emerged as a stockier cat, with small rounded ears while the Angora remained a long-bodied, slender breed with tall ears.

Persians have a lifespan of 10-18 years, with most living past 15 years.

In general they are hardy cats, but there are potential health problems, most relative to the flattened facial features. I address Persian health fully in Chapter 9 and discuss potential genetic conditions that can appear with this breed.

Types of Persian Cats

In England, each color of Persian is regarded as a separate breed, while in America, the Persian is a single breed with many color variations. For the purpose of simplicity, I'll describe the "types" of Persian by color.

I regard the cats as representative of a single breed, with more than 150 color combinations possible.

Chocolate/lilacs are the only color where BOTH parents have to possess the gene in order to produce a visual of that color. That's why they are rare and usually more expensive.

The following are the major color divisions recognized in the cat fancy.

Solid or Self

Persians that are "selfs" have a solid color that is the same throughout their coat in an even tone of blue, black, chocolate, lilac, cream, white, and red.

The "blues" are a deep shade of gray while the "lilac" tone is much warmer. Reds are ginger or copper, while the chocolate is a rich brown. Black Persians are just that, pitch black, while the whites are the color of milk.

Tortoiseshell

The Tortoiseshell Persian or "Tortie" is a cat with a two-color coat of intermingled or mottled colors with very little white. The color mixes most commonly seen are cream, blue, black, red, lilac, and chocolate. Those that are tortoiseshell and white are often referred to as calico in America.

All variations of "Torties" have intense copper eyes.

Color Point

Color point Persians have darker markings on their extremities, in particular the ears, face, legs, and tail. The coloration is the result of crossing Persians with Siamese cats, a breed famous for the pointed marking.

In America, the Color Point Persian is referred to as the Himalayan. In order of popularity the color combinations include Seal Point with dark brown/black markings, Blue

Point, Flame Point (red), Tortie Point, Cream Point, the rare Lilac Point and Chocolate Points with milk chocolate markings, and the exotic Lynx Points and Bi-Color Points.

Lynx Points and Bi-Colors are not considered rare but they are uncommon, and the least-requested, mainly because most people are unfamiliar with them.

All variations have bright and vivid blue eyes.

The cross with the Siamese gives the Himalayan the characteristics of both breeds, namely docile, gentle, and affectionate like the Persian with the sparkly, outgoing, friendly traits of the Siamese. They are a bit more active than Persians and are very people-oriented. They will usually follow you from room to room or be quite content to lie on your lap or right next to you and purr away.

Himalayans just want to be wherever you are and can be a little bit needy. They enjoy being the center of attention and are almost dog-like and will greet strangers at the door looking to be "pet" or to just say "hello." Because they are social animals they are happiest with a feline companion (or a dog) to keep company and play with; therefore getting more exercise.

A Himalayan cat left alone all day will suffer loneliness and may become depressed, pining for its owner. This is a beautiful breed and its personality and temperament make it an outstanding companion animal.

Above: Himalayan Seal Points
Photo Credit: Joan of KaristaKats

Tabby Patterns

Tabby Persians have coats that are light with dark spots, marbling or stripes in three distinct variations:

Tiger of Mackerel Tabby — The stripes run from the spine and around the body at a 90 degree angle.

Marbled Tabby — This is a more blotched pattern characterized by wide stripes curving over the body interrupted with "bull's eye" markings on the sides and flanks.

Patched — This pattern is typified by large round spots that are distributed evenly over the cat's body.

These patterns can appear on a variety of base coat colors including, blue, silver, cream, red, brown, and resulting combinations like blue-silver or silver-cream.

Most of these cats have copper eyes, although Tabby Persians with silver coats usually have green or hazel eyes.

Bi-Color

You will sometimes see Bi-Color Persians referred to as Harlequins or Parti-Colors because they are a combination of white with one other color appearing in dark patches.

These distinctions can be quite precise according to the ratio of white to black, a fact that really only interests breeders trying to achieve precise genetic mixes. You'll just see a gorgeous Persian that is a pleasing combination of white with red, black, blue, chocolate, lilac, or cream patches.

All will have copper eyes, although there are breeding programs that are trying to selectively incorporate blue and odd-eyed Bi-Color varieties.

Smoke and Shaded

In Smoke and Shaded Persians the coat appears to be a solid color, but when the cat moves, or the hair is parted, a white undercoat is exposed.

In the Smokes, approximately 50%-80% of each individual hair shaft is colored, while the root is a white to silver color. The effect is simply stunning.

If only the upper third of the hair is colored with the rest displaying the light or white coloration, the cat is said to be Shaded.

All variations have copper eyes.

Chinchilla

The Chinchilla Persian is a cat with an undercoat that is snow white or silver with black tipping on the head, ears, back, sides, and tail. Only the tips of the hairs in these locations are colored.

The Chinchilla Persian was the pet of the evil villain 'Blofeld' in the James Bond movies.

Above: Chinchilla Silver Persian
Photo Credit: Molly Barr of Mythicbells Persians

The Golden Chinchilla is an extremely rare variation of this marking, with a warm cream or apricot where the black tipping is normally found.

The eyes, which are rimmed in black, will be either green or blue-green.

There is even a Blue Golden, and breeder Carole Gainsbury explains how this came about:

"I have been breeding Persians since 1984 and started showing which led me into becoming a full Persian judge for the GCCF in the United Kingdom.

I began breeding Chinchilla and Goldens in the 1990s, venturing into the blue series by putting my Golden Female to my Grand Champion Red Tabby male — both carried the dilute gene. I found I had bred the first Blue Golden male called Caszan Blue Thunder.

I feel the Blue Series have wonderful coat colors, the Blue Golden's look is very striking with a wheat-colored contrast to the blue with good green eyes. Introducing an outcross gene produces lovely natures with good boning."

Grooming Requirements

The grooming requirements of the Persian are sufficiently significant that I am devoting an entire chapter to the topic.

This is, in my mind, the major adoption consideration. You must be prepared to appropriately care for a long-haired cat.

In addition to reading the chapter on grooming, which at minimum means daily combing and monthly visits to a professional groomer, I recommend that you spend some time online watching videos of Persians being groomed.

While many of these videos are produced by professionals, and involve equipment and procedures you yourself might not perform, they will give you an appreciation for the density of the Persian coat.

The primary task in grooming is to keep the coat free of oil and grit, as well as preventing tangles and mats. This can only be done with DAILY attention.

Do not think you can get away with less. It's not fair to the cat. Matted and tangled fur is unsightly, unhealthy and painful for the cat.

Persian Personality

Persians are not powerhouses of energy. In fact, I can't really imagine a hyperactive Persian. The mental image just will not form for me. This is not to say that they can't be playful and fun.

Persians love to invent games with their humans, but the play is always gentle and interspersed with long periods of doing what Persians do best — arranging themselves in an elegant spot and being beautiful.

I have often said that my cats know that when I bring out the camera that it's time for "hair and make-up" to start. I won't go so far as to say they've ever looked at me and said, "This is my best side," but they are highly skilled at positioning themselves to the best possible advantage.

Beyond what can only be called just a bit of vanity, these cats are so lovely and sweet-tempered that it's impossible not to be calm in their presence.

They are devoted to humans, although often just a bit selective with their affections. I do not have children, but I have had many opportunities to observe Persians around youngsters.

The Persian as a Family Cat

These are not contentious cats, and they will do fine with well-mannered children. If the cat doesn't like what's going on, he simply removes himself. I believe that all children should be taught to deal respectfully and gently with animals.

Any cat, no matter how well-behaved, will react if it is being handled roughly or harassed. That's simply in the animal's nature.

In those situations, I frankly think it is the child that needs to be instructed in better behavior, not the cat. Of course extra care is required for very young children (under the age of 5) as they will be unaware of the potential damage they can cause a young kitten.

Be sure to teach your children how best to lift up a cat with one hand just behind the front legs, while the other hand takes the weight by supporting his hindquarters.

Your Persian will enjoy being held, although usually only for a short time and on their terms. Stroke him while holding him, as this provides reassurance. Once he struggles, be sure to lower him quickly or prepare to be bitten or scratched!

When starting to stroke, begin from the head to the tail, along the back, and stop at the tail. Scratching under the chin or on top the head between the ears are favorite places.

All in all, however, Persians make fine family cats, generally performing more of an observational role than a participatory one.

Persians and Other Pets

Not surprisingly, Persians do quite well with other pets, including dogs — again, so long as Fido is well behaved. They will not thrive in a house where a dog is constantly harassing or chasing them.

Although cats will be cats, Persians are not as likely to go after the family parakeet or "fish" in the aquarium as other breeds. In multi-species households, I recommend careful segregation. Tightly latched cages and secure aquarium lids make for good neighbors.

Initially you should supervise the introduction, especially if you have a dog. A kitten may likely claw at a dog's face and make him aggressive. Let the animals learn each other's scent first and get 'comfortable' with each other before you dare leave them alone together.

Multiple Persians

Multiple Persians will live quite happily together, especially if the two cats were acquired at the same time. The only issue with keeping more than one Persian is the amount of work you will have to do as well as possible increased scratching and spraying if you have three or more.

Remember that these long-haired cats will have to be combed every day for 5-15 minutes each, and will, at the least, have to be groomed by a professional once a month. If you are prepared to meet these needs for one or more Persians, you'll have no difficulty keeping multiples as "roomies."

Male or Female?

This is a standard question, and one I'm frankly not sure has any validity with this breed. It's possible that female Persians are somewhat more independent, but I really do not see a lot of difference in the personality and temperament of the genders.

All Persians are extremely calm and even-tempered. They're all a bit given to being couch potatoes, and once the males are altered, this is even more the case.

In my opinion, since spraying is rarely if ever an issue with neutered males, selecting the gender of your pet is purely a matter of personal preference on your part, or availability of adoptable kittens.

Similar Breeds

The Turkish Angora is also a highly popular long-haired cat, but with a longer nose and wedge-shaped head when compared to the rounded profile and short nose of the Persian.

Angoras have almond eyes rather than round, and a more Oriental appearance. They are long, slender cats with plumed tails. Standing side by side, it's clear that the Persian is a more muscular cat with a squarish set to the body standing on short legs.

Angoras are quite handsome in their own right and if you want a long-haired cat but don't like the flattened facial features of the Persian, this is an excellent choice.

Persian Pros and Cons

Obviously people want a summary of pros and cons of any breed they are considering, but I don't think that's an easy discussion with any type of animal.

For instance, I love dogs. I was raised around Yorkshire Terriers, and they're fantastic, feisty little souls, but I wouldn't want a dog for the simple reason that I don't want to walk one all the time.

My "dog" friends, however, wax eloquent about how much they love their outings with their pets to the park or out in the country. Me? I'd rather change a litter box and be done with it.

Obviously, I think Persians are wonderful cats. They have superior personalities and the most laid-back demeanor imaginable. They are absolute creatures of habit, and will adjust very nicely to your schedule without going through a lot of separation anxiety.

They're not loud, insistent, or demanding. They have a nice feel to them, being much stockier than most people realize. I like big-bodied, heavy cats, so a lap full of Persian suits me just fine.

Most live to around 15 years of age, and unless they are susceptible to some genetic defects involving their eyes and nose, tend to be healthy pets. I've had quite good luck with mine in this aspect of ownership.

Obviously then, the most evident argument against owning a Persian is their long hair. If you aren't going to comb your Persian daily and engage the services of a professional groomer regularly, I'd recommend you consider a short-haired breed.

Daily grooming takes at least 5-15 minutes to be effective, and this is not an area where you can or should scrimp in your feline husbandry practices. It's not a chore I've ever minded. In fact, I find it relaxing, but some people see combing a cat as a deal breaker.

Many years ago I lived in a townhouse complex while caring for an elderly relative. Our next door neighbor had a Persian that was basically one great big tangled mat of hair.

I stood it as long as I could and finally volunteered to pay for the animal to be professionally groomed as a "Christmas present." It was actually more of an intervention on the animal's behalf.

When the groomer shaved all that hair off, the poor cat had developed sores due to lack of air circulation to the skin.

The "Christmas present" turned out to be a monthly thing, on my dime, until the owner was forced to go into a nursing home and the cat went to a new home where daily grooming was dutifully performed.

Grooming isn't just a cosmetic chore, it's an aspect of proper health care for your pet. If you can't meet that obligation, a Persian is not for you.

But, apart from these considerations, I don't really see a lot of "cons" to owning a Persian. There's a good reason why they are the most popular of all cat breeds in North America and equally as popular in Europe and the UK — they're great cats!

Chapter 2 - Finding a Persian Breeder

Finding a cat to adopt is not a problem. There are hundreds of thousands of homeless animals in need of loving care, which is why I always advocate rescue adoptions. This is not to discourage potential cat owners from seeking a pedigreed animal, and certainly not to suggest that you shouldn't adopt a Persian.

Like all other aspects of living with a companion animal, however, you have to know why you want a pedigreed cat and why you specifically want a Persian, which is the topic I addressed in the first chapter. Pedigreed cats are not that different from any other sort of cat except that they have a verifiable family tree that goes back 4-5 generations.

Such animals can be registered with cat associations. They qualify as exemplars of a given breed because most can "breed true," meaning that when you mate a Persian male with a Persian female, the kittens will look like their parents.

Such factors that come under consideration when judging a cat to be a true representation of a designated breed include color, pattern, length of the coat, texture of the coat, and body type. This last is further divided into the shape of the head, and type and set of the ears and eyes. Tail length is also relevant as is overall temperament and personality.

Breeders work toward the recognized "breed standard," which is the generally accepted list of requirements necessary for perfection in any breed group. This is also the basis for judging the animals competitively in organized cat shows.

You will need to decide whether to look for an adult cat or kitten. So what are the differences?

Well, of course kittens are cute, small and very playful. But they can also be curious in terms of scratching your lovely furniture and climbing up the curtains!

They really are like having a baby or small child — they need lots of attention and looking after. An adult has already been through these 'growing pains' and so you will have a lot less socialization and adjustments to deal with, although the downside is that they may have ingrained 'bad' habits which are hard if not impossible to change at this stage.

Pet Quality vs. Show Quality

Due to the costs associated with purebred adoptions, most people who simply want a beautiful companion will only be able to afford a "pet quality" kitten from a recognized cattery.

These are kittens that, for reasons that are largely inconsequential to people outside the cat fancy, don't conform precisely enough to the breed standard to be used in a breeding program.

They are sold to qualified candidates at a lower price with the express provision that they be spayed or neutered. This protects the cattery's bloodlines and prevents the passing on of undesirable traits.

Understanding the World of Catteries

With this understanding of the world of pedigreed cats, you should be able to understand clearly that professional catteries are not one-stop kitten shops.

There is a definite process involved in purchasing a pedigreed cat, and it may be a protracted one. You must understand from the beginning that you are contracting to adopt a living creature from a breeder who has dedicated a large portion of their life to caring for their cats, selectively cultivating their cattery's bloodline as a premier representation of the breed.

You don't want to deal with a breeder who exhibits any less than that degree of commitment, nor do you want to deal with an operation that even suggests you can just walk in, put your money on the counter, and walk out with a cat. That is a kitten mill, not a professional cattery, and not an operation whose activities any true cat lover wants to support.

This is a situation where money does not necessary "talk." I have known of many instances where prospective buyers have been turned away from a cattery, and I, myself have declined to allow certain candidates to adopt one of my kittens.

If I cannot be completely assured that one of my cats will go to a loving and attentive home where all of its needs will be met, there is no amount of money a person can put in front of me that will persuade me to agree to the adoption.

I also strongly believe that the adoption of a pedigree cat is a two-way exchange. I expect to answer specific questions and to ask them. I always politely explain that I am not attempting to give people the third-degree, but that I must have assurances about the safety and care of the cat. On the rare occasions when a potential buyer has become offended, I have terminated the negotiations.

In response, I am happy to provide references and maintain a list of former clients and colleagues who will discuss working with me and living with my cats. A breeder who will not provide references to you, and by this, I mean people who are willing to be contacted, would, in my opinion, not be someone you'd want to deal with.

Locating and Evaluating Breeders

I was already a life-long cat lover when I became interested in Persians, so I was aware of the necessary steps to locate a breeder and negotiate for an adoption. On the whole, you should have no difficulty finding a Persian breeder as these cats are incredibly popular as companion animals.

Attend Cat Shows

Personally, I think the best way to locate a professional breeder with a good reputation is to visit cat shows. You will be looking for someone who has real expertise with the Persian breed.

The best breeders are not motivated by profit alone. These breeders will most likely show their cats. A lot of people think that showing is a beauty contest, but it's really a lot more than that. The people that show are interested in keeping the breed looking like it should but also do extensive health testing and genetic research to keep the breed stable.

Cat shows check all of this before giving titles, because the titles are a reflection of the commitment each breeder has made to protecting and preserving the breed.

A cat with a title is confirmed by CFA/TICA to be a good representation of the breed and breeders with multiple titles on their cats show that they have the knowledge and the experience to contribute to the breed, and not destroy it.

The higher the titles on the cat, the more experienced and dedicated the breeder of that cat is.

In the chapter on showing cats, I will discuss the atmosphere and workings of a cat show in greater length.

Cat shows are excellent places to look at beautiful cats and to collect business cards from catteries.

A cat show is not, however, the place to negotiate for the purchase of a kitten. The atmosphere is very hectic, and the venue is not intended for that kind of business activity.

Think of attending a cat show as "window shopping." There, you will see catteries displaying their premier animals. Certainly you can ask questions of the exhibitors, and it's perfectly acceptable to say, "May I have your business card? I'd like to contact you to talk about your cats." Don't say, "I want to buy one of your cats."

You can ask about current availability and the proposed breeding schedule for the year. Really well run catteries schedule litters carefully, so you'll be able to judge when you might be able to adopt.

When you can arrange a lengthier conversation by phone, or in person, there are some definite things you want to find out from the breeder.

Information the Breeder Should Supply

When you visit a cattery for the first time, you are going to be subject to what I call the "awwwww" factor. It's very hard to treat the visit as a business transaction when you're surrounded by gorgeous cats and excited about the process of taking one home to be your companion for many years to come.

Since I melt at the sight of Persian kittens with their fluffy round heads and big innocent eyes, I completely understand this. For that reason, I have always answered a lot of questions for my clients before they even ask, but you can't trust every breeder to do that.

Prepare a list of questions in advance. At the least, you want to cover the following points and areas of discussion.

Getting Information About the Cattery

Find out how long the breeder has been in operation. With what breeds are they working now in addition to the Persian, and with what breeds have they worked in the past?

If you did not meet the breeder at a cat show, ask if they exhibit their animals and ask why or why not, depending on the answer you receive.

How large is the breeding operation at the cattery? The best operations are those that maintain a manageable population of cats so that socialization of the kittens is not only possible, but a high priority.

Some warning signs that you are not dealing with a reputable breeder include:

- A basic lack of knowledge about the breed that is apparent through evasive and vague answers.

- Complete denial that the breed is prone to any genetic defects or assurances that such defects are impossible in the cats they raise.

- An obvious lack of involvement with the cats.

- Refusal or reticence to let you tour the cattery and meet and interact with the cats.

- An inability or unwillingness to produce various forms of documentation regarding ancestry and health.

- Brushes off the importance of socialization saying all cats "have to adjust" or "will get used to" whatever they encounter.

Information About the Breeding Pair

Find out as much information as you can about the kittens' parents. Have they been healthy? How many litters has the female produced? Who is the father? Why was he chosen as part of the breeding pair?

Ask to see the parents' health records and actually look at them. Check for routine visits to the veterinarian, the regular administration of vaccinations, and any tests or procedures that have been performed. If you see words or phrases you don't understand, make notes and discuss them with your own vet, or look them up online.

Ask to meet and interact with the parents. While this is not always an accurate representation of the temperament you can expect your new kitten to exhibit, it's a pretty fair test.

Current State of the Kitten's Health

Ask what kind of care the mother received while she was carrying the kittens. How were they delivered? Was it a normal birth? Have the kittens been nursing routinely? Have they needed any medical care? If so, for what? Has there been any problem with fleas or worms?
Are they old enough to have received any vaccinations? If so, what shots have been administered? Will you be provided with a copy of all of the health records when you take possession of the cat?

Always ask about the health guarantee that is part of the adoption agreement and make sure that you fully understand its provisions.

The Issue of Genetic Health Conditions

Because Persians have a short, flattened face and nose, the breed commonly suffers from breathing issues, including shortness of breath. They can also be subject to dental misalignments or malocclusions that make it difficult for them to pick up food.

If a Persian's tear ducts are malformed, the cat can suffer from epiphora, the overflowing of tears onto the face. This problem, though cosmetic in nature, is still one that should be mentioned by a forthcoming breeder.

It is also possible for Persians to suffer from eyelid malformations that cause the eyelashes to rub against the cornea resulting in damage and infection.

The incidence of polycystic kidney disease is about 49% with Persians. I'll discuss this condition fully in the chapter on health, but again, a reputable breeder will be very upfront with this information. They should also mention the potential for hypertrophic cardiomyopathy, progressive retinal atrophy, hip dysplasia, and basal cell carcinomas among others.

While many of these conditions can occur in cats of all breeds, a higher than usual incidence among Persians makes them worthy of discussion.

An honest breeder will tell you how often these problems have surfaced in their kittens, but they will not tell you that their line is completely free of genetic defects. That is absolutely impossible, and is not a guarantee you should be offered or that you should accept.

Methods of Socialization Used

Socialization is a vitally important topic to explore with a breeder. Typically kittens remain at a cattery until they're about 3 months old. During that time, they will be trained to use both a litter box and a scratching post. Until those skills are mastered and they have been weaned from their mother, the babies are not eligible for adoption.

Although sometimes kittens are adopted from as early as six weeks of age, you should be aware that this is not ideal and potentially harmful. You may end up with a scared and nervous kitten that hides away a lot.

Conscientious breeders have specific methods to make sure that their kittens are well-socialized. This includes lots of handling on a daily basis, and the opportunity to explore and interact with other cats. Kittens need a great deal of intellectual stimulation to keep their curious and bright minds occupied.

Ideally, there will also be some reasonable and supervised exposure to other animals, primarily dogs, children, and a degree of normal household and environmental noise. If exposed to these factors at an early age, cats tend to be less reactive and anxious as adults, and in general more adaptable.

Persians have a long-standing reputation for being sweet-natured and placid. I've always been amused by the way mine seem to find the place in the house that sets them off to their best advantage before proceeding to lounge all afternoon in beautifully placed languor. As a breed, therefore, nervousness is usually not an issue with a Persian, but this doesn't negate the need for sound socialization at a young age.

The Questions You Should Be Asked

As I indicated, since it's perfectly possible to be turned down by a cattery, you should expect to answer a series of questions about yourself and your lifestyle. Whenever I go through this process, I am not prying, but I do need to be able to make a judgment about the home to which my kittens will be going.

Persians are not what I would call needy cats, but they do crave the love and attention of their humans even if they don't harass you the way a determined and vocal Siamese would.

I ask if the potential Persian "parent" has previous experience with cats, and if so, what breed or breeds. I'm especially concerned that potential adopters understand the grooming needs of a long-haired cat like a Persian.

I pay special attention to the questions I receive in return. If I raise the issue of grooming and the person does not begin trying to learn more about caring for a Persian's coat, I take that as a red flag. I promise you that every breeder who is passionate about their cats can spot someone trying to lie to them in a heartbeat.

I ask where the kitten will sleep, and who will care for the Persian in the owner's absence for vacation or work-based travel commitments. I want to know if they have an existing veterinarian, and if they don't, I offer a list of clinics in the area.

Photo Credit: Molly Barr of Mythicbells Persians

Because I am perfectly willing to be a resource for my clients after the adoption, and because I call to check on the kitten periodically in the first few months, I want to establish a friendly rapport.

The response and level of receptiveness I get from the person with whom I'm dealing tells me a lot. Sometimes, if the whole thing just doesn't feel right, I do say no.

Chapter 3 - Closing the Deal

Now, for as businesslike as the adoption of a pedigreed cat should be, the best part is that you are going to meet some adorable Persian kittens!

Before you can play with the babies, you'll probably be asked to use hand sanitizer. This is for their protection, not yours. Many feline diseases are highly communicable, so sanitation precautions are necessary. This is a good sign that you are dealing with a knowledgeable breeder.

Don't just be swept away by the adorable cuteness — and unbelievable softness — of a baby Persian. You do need to pay attention to some particulars about the kitten's condition as you lapse into baby talk and start picking out names.

The Coat

Persian kittens have absolutely luscious fur that should be completely intact, with no missing patches, and no matting. The baby should feel and smell clean.

Gently blow on the coat to part it a little so you can see the skin. It should be healthy in appearance with no drying or flaking. This is also a good time to gently turn the baby over on its back and have a look at the "armpits" and under the tail.

Finding Fleas

If the baby has "passengers" as I prefer to call fleas, those are the areas where they will be most evident. If you do find a flea or two, it really isn't a deal breaker, or necessarily a commentary on the quality of the cattery. Fleas represent an ongoing battle for breeders, and if the local climate is warm year round, it's even worse.

The important thing is that the baby not be overrun with fleas because then the blood loss could be sufficient to cause anemia. If fleas are present, you want to take care of that before you take the baby home. I am categorically against all forms of chemical flea control no matter how "safe" they are supposed to be.

If you find fleas, ask the breeder to bathe the kitten prior to adoption and immediately begin using a fine tooth flea comb with the baby as soon as you get home. Wash all the kitten's bedding on a daily basis for a week or two just to ensure that no eggs are being laid by any surviving fleas.

The Eyes

Baby Persians have heartbreakingly sweet round eyes with a bright, innocent expression. The gaze should be curious and interested. Make sure there is no evidence of any kind of runny discharge.

Take this opportunity to discuss tearing with the breeder. Running eyes and tear stains are a problem with this breed. I'll discuss this more fully in the chapter on daily care, but the owner of the cattery should have some advice to offer about dealing with the problem.

This question is less an issue of getting the advice than a subtle way to find out just how involved the breeder is in the daily lives of the cats.

The Nose

Persian cats are prone to developing sinus issues and having breathing problems due to their flattened facial features and nose. Kittens that are already displaying these problems, or that are having labored breathing so early in life could have chronic issues.

Again, I would not necessarily say this is a deal-breaker, but I would ask for an independent evaluation of the kitten by a veterinarian who has experience with the Persian breed. There really is no way to predict if this will be a problem in any individual cat. I've had Persians with sinus and seasonal allergies, and others that never exhibited a single sign of such issues.

Negotiating the Terms of the Adoption

When both you and the breeder are satisfied that an adoption will proceed, you will be asked to sign a written contract. All catteries have their own adoption agreements, but there are some standard features you will encounter.

Initial Health Evaluation

Typically the contract will stipulate that within 48-72 hours of your taking possession of the cat, you will take your new pet to a qualified veterinarian for evaluation.

This provides a baseline measure of the kitten's health should it become necessary to invoke the agreement's health guarantee for any reason. The breeder will ask that you supply written proof of your compliance with this stipulated vet visit.

Spaying or Neutering Requirement

When adopting a pet quality animal from a reputable cattery, you will be required to have your pet spayed or neutered before it reaches six months of age. When you provide written proof that the procedure has been performed, you will receive the cat's final papers.

This is a measure to protect the integrity of the cattery's bloodlines, and to ensure that more unwanted pets are not brought into a world where companion animal homelessness already stands at shocking levels.

Prohibition Against Declawing

Frankly, I would be suspicious of any adoption agreement for a cat that does not include strong language about the inhumane practice of declawing. This hideous practice is illegal in Europe, and in many parts of the United States, as well it should be.

While "declawing" may sound benign enough, in reality, this procedure necessitates the amputation of the last digit of the toe. It is terribly painful for the cat, and negatively affects its mobility for life, while depriving the animal of its primary and natural means of self-defense.

Persians are not given to vigorous clawing, but that is beside the point. Any cat can be easily trained to behave appropriately with its claws if provided with proper scratching apparatus early on.

The radical surgical removal of the claws is, in my opinion, a move designed for the callous convenience of the owner. It is, in no way, a move designed to support the well-being of the cat.

If I sound like I'm on a soap box, I am. If you are even contemplating having a Persian or any other breed of cat declawed, you need to rethink your choice of pet.

Agreement Basics

As you review the adoption agreement, the basic provisions and terms should include:

- A general description of the Persian breed.
- A description of the specific animal you are adopting in terms of color and any patterning.
- The gender of the kitten being adopted.
- The names of the breeding pair.
- The agreed-upon price of the kitten.
- Any stipulations for release of the final papers.

- The contact information of both parties making the agreement.

Other stipulations may include your agreement to:

- Provide appropriate and ongoing health care in concert with a qualified veterinary professional including the administration of recommended vaccinations.

- Your understanding of the grooming needs of the breed in question and assurance that all necessary and appropriate grooming will be performed.

- Contact the breeder should you ever be faced with the necessity of giving up the cat.

This last point is something that I make sure to emphasize to anyone who adopts one of my cats. Every breeder I know feels the same way about this. None of us want to see our cats wind up in a bad living situation or, worse yet, a shelter.

If you have to give up a pedigreed animal you have purchased, contact the breeder! I will always take back one of my cats under this circumstance and either keep the animal or find a way to place it in a new home.

If I am going to take a cat back, I do require that it be tested for FELV/FIV, fecal parasites, and ringworm before I take possession. This is simply to safeguard my other cats before reintroducing the individual into the population.

Consider Persian Rescue Groups

Heaven knows I melt at the sight of a Persian kitten. I love everything about raising them. While Persian babies grow up to be lovely and placid, they are capable of being just as rowdy as any other kind of kitten.

There have been plenty of times when I've had one climbing up my leg, another turning over a pot plant, and the third cascading litter out on to the carpet only to ask myself, "Why do I do this?" Then they all stop and look at me, and I know why I do it.

But, as joyous as raising a kitten may be, I have also adopted many rescue animals in my years of being a "crazy cat lady."

Two of my current cats are crossbreed Russian Blues that were abandoned at birth at a vet clinic. They came to me when they were 11 months old and are simply outstanding cats.

The great popularity of the Persian breed means there are many purchased each year as pets by people who really do not know what is involved in caring for a long-haired cat.

Far too many of these same animals are turned over to shelters when their owners tire of them. In other instances, the cats may be abandoned because an elderly owner has passed away or a family has fallen on hard times and can no longer afford to keep a pet.

All rescue animals are in need of a "forever home." Of course I'm crazy about Persians, but if you are simply looking for a loving companion, please always consider a shelter adoption. It is not hyperbole to say that you will be saving a life.

Even if you do not go this route, please consider making a donation to your local no-kill shelter or volunteering to help their efforts in some way. Animal shelters are always in desperate need of funds, supplies, and volunteers.

These people and their generous supporters provide a vital function in the cause for animal welfare and are, to my eyes, some of the kindest and most dedicated folk you will ever meet.

What Do Persians Cost?

Pedigreed Persians are not inexpensive cats. Depending on the specific type in which you are interested, expect to pay anywhere from $3000-$5000 / £1838-£3063 for a pedigreed Persian of pet quality and $5000+ / £3063+ for a show quality animal.

(Please note that prices vary widely by cattery and bloodline.)

Obviously, the average cat owner will not be able to meet these prices. Due to the popularity of the breed, it is common to obtain kittens from enthusiast breeders who may simply be allowing a female to raise a litter before she is spayed.

Typically Persians acquired under these or similar circumstances sell for about $600 / £350. If kittens are offered at a substantially lower rate with the claim that they are Persians, I doubt seriously that the animals are purebred.

The last thing anyone wants to do is to encourage the operation of kitten mills. There is a difference between an enthusiast breeder offering five to six kittens for adoption and someone who says they routinely have Persian kittens at a cut rate.

Be careful of what we call "for profit" breeders. They pick the lowest quality cats and breed the kittens for a profit, leading to many cats that end up in rescue or with very short life spans. The cats rarely look like Persians and look more like Maine Coons, Ragdolls, or just plain old alley cats.

Beware of breeders who suggest you check back in a few weeks. Responsible owners will not allow their female cats to have more than one or two litters per year. You are more likely to be put on a waiting list at a legitimate cattery than to be told kittens will be available shortly.

Be suspicious of any adoption that is treated as an immediate cash sale. If it's a legitimate sale you can expect to be interviewed with a heavy emphasis on your suitability to provide an appropriate home for the cat.

Chapter 4 - Persian Catteries in the US

Agape Persians
Nina Papageorge
Cell: 562.760.2006
Email: ninapapa@cox.net
www.agapepersian.com

Beaukit Cattery
Barbara and Larry Bouchelle
Phone: 972-247-2147
Email: bouchel@sbcglobal.net
www.beaukit.com

Bella Mia
Heather Colbert
Northern California
Email: colbertheather@hotmail.com
www.bellamiacattery.com

By Heavenly
Brenda Morton
4697 Morton Road
Sutton, WV, 26601
Phone: 304-619-1429
Email: brenda59@mtn-air.net
www.heavensentpersians.com

Catortionist
Central New Jersey
Email: info@catortionist.com
www.catortionist.com

Cherishabuls
Email: cathy@cherishabuls.com
www.cherishabuls.com

Cleokat Persians
Pat Gallagher
Southern California near San Diego
Phone: 619 453-7858
Email: cleokat@yahoo.com
www.cleokat.com

Crayola Cats
Julie Beeman
South Carolina
Cell: 954-662-4099
Home: 541-577-3231
Email: Julie@craycats.com
www.craycats.com

Cuddle Paws
Debbie Evans
Bloomsburg, Pennsylvania
Email: duke1321@ptd.net
www.cuddlepaws.com

Dazzle M
Ardell Sims
Sacramento, California
Phone: 916-991-6530
Email: dazzlekits@aol.com
www.dazzle-m.com

DiRose Cattery
Jacksonville, Florida
Email: himis@di-rose.com
www.di-rose.com

Dreamquete Exotics, Persians, & JBTs
Email: dreamquete@yahoo.com
www.dreamquete.com

Exotic Den
Dennis Sanders
Southern California
Phone: 562.427.1093
Email: SANDERS901@aol.com
www.exoticden.com

HunnyDew Persians
Denver, Colorado
Karen Dewey
Email: karen@hunnydewpersians.com
www.hunnydewpersians.com

KaristaKats Himalayans
Joan Donahue-Ulmer
Califon, New Jersey
Phone: 908-832-9188
Email: karistakats@comcast.net
www.karistakats.com

Karkens Cattery
Fairless Hills, Pennsylvania
Phone: 215-945-2775
Email: KARKENS@AOL.COM
www.karkenscattery.com

Last Call Cattery
Alpharetta, GA
Lynn (Mostowy) Lopiano
Phone: 404.513.0204
Email: lastcallcattery@bellsouth.net
www.lastcallcattery.com

Little Angel Cats
Phone: (707) 344-5550 or (707) 688-2848
Email: persiangreeneyes@comcast.net
Internet: http://littleangelcats.com/

Loknglas Exotic Shorthairs & Persians
Email: loknglascats@aol.com
www.loknglas.com

Lushell Persians
Dumfries, VA 22025
Phone: 203-670-2385
Email: lushellcats@gmail.com
www.lushell.com

Meow House
Shannon McGraw
Phone: 214-264-7261
Email: shannon@meowhousekittens.com
www.meowhousekittens.com

Mythicbells Persians
Molly Barr
Email: persians@mythicbells.com
www.mythicbells.com

Napa Valley Persians
Gina Imrie
Phone: 707-287-2958
Email: ginadware@aol.com
www.napavalleypersians.com

Parti Wai Ex
Penni and Jon Richter
951/787-6260
California — USA
Email: pbrichter@earthlink.net
www.partiwaiex.com/

Purfect Gift Cattery
Email: judy@purfectgift.com
www.purfectgift.com

PuffStuff Cattery
Dr. Konstantin E. Voronin,
Mt. Pleasant, SC, USA
Phone: 843-856-2852

E-mail: puffstuffcats@hotmail.com
www.puffstuffcats.com

Purfurvid
Email: jeanne@purfurvid.com
www.purfurvid.com

Purrpals
P.O. Box 3976
Citrus Heights, CA 95611-3976
Email: Purrpals@aol.com
www.purrpals.info

Rarebreed Cattery
Email: Amber@RarebreedCattery.com
www.rarebreedcattery.com

RB Cat House
Rhonda Baerwald
850 S. Hwy 59
Sulphur Springs, AR
Phone: 479-298-9898
Cell: 479-787-8414
Email: persian.baby@yahoo.com
www.persianbabys.com

Sejumay
Debbie & Pat Kenny
Email: debbie@sejumay.com
www.sejumay.com

Shadow Oak Persians
Terri Lyn Alexander
Email: shadowoakcattery@aol.com
www.shadowoakpersians.com

Sybil Persians
Sybil Bruckman
Pennsylvania
Email: sybil@ptd.net
www.sybilcats.com

Windy Valley Persians
Murrieta, California
Kelley Phillips
Email: peekaboopersians@aol.com
www.windyvalleypersians.com

Winnplace Cattery
Phone: 239-810-0066
Email: WinnnplaceCattery@aol.com
www.winnplacecattery.com

Vanleigh Persians
Email: vanleigh@bellsouth.net
www.vanleighpersians.com

Zafiro
Matthew Martin
Phone: 505-453-6853
Email: info@zafiropersians.com
http://www.zafiropersians.com

Chapter 5 - Persian Catteries in the UK

Algernon Persians
Margaret & Eric Charlan
Telephone: 01706 750548
Email: eandm1@sky.com
www.algernonpersians.co.uk

Caszan Persians
Carole Gainsbury
Tel/Fax 01932 240215
Email: info@caszan.com
www.caszan.co.uk

Falabella Persians
Kate Howard
Tel: 07751 836671
www.falabellapersians.co.uk

Gemkin Persians
Jenny Nicholas
Tel Home: UK   01745 890519
Tel Mobile: UK   07813 713820
International — 44 1745 890519
Email: jenny@gemkinpersians.com
www.gemkinpersians.com

Khatynka
Mary Rollerson
Wisbech
Cambs/Norfolk borders
Tel: 01945 871191
Email: mary@khatynka.co.uk
www.khatynka.co.uk

Mystere Persians
Diane Hunt
Chelmsford, Essex UK
Tel No. 01245 604567
Int. Tel. No +44 1245 604567
Email: mysterecats@gmail.com
www.mysterepersians.co.uk

Palchinno Persians
Rose & David Angus
Email: info@palchinnopersians.co.uk
Tel: 01993 842727
www.palchinnopersians.co.uk

Riascatz
Email: marie.hill@yahoo.co.uk
www.riascatzpersians.com

Chapter 6 - Daily Care for Your Persian

When people consider a specific breed of cat for adoption, they immediately want to know about the personality, as if every individual will behave exactly the same way. This truly is not the case.

Cats are very individualistic, and they are influenced by the manner in which they were raised and the environment in which they are currently living.

Some Thoughts on Persian Personality

I can offer you some selective insights on living with a Persian, but I strongly encourage you not to go into a relationship with any companion animal with preset expectations. Let your friendship with your new pet evolve naturally, and don't try to force any reactions.

Selective With Their Affection

Although some cat breeds do have a reputation for being highly social, I have found that in most cases cats will single out one person as the object of their affection. This is especially true with Persians.

When you have earned their trust and love, they are absolutely devoted and thoroughly enjoy being fussed over by their human. In fact, they can even get a little snitty with you if they think they aren't getting enough attention.

But if a Persian doesn't like you all that much, you'll be confronted with a beautiful cat that holds itself aloof and a bit distant. It's very rare for a Persian to become hostile to the point of aggression, but they are masters of the art of ignoring you as if you did not exist.

Cats are Not Loners

As a breed, Persians do not suffer from separation anxiety, nor will they hound your every step for attention. They can do quite well on their own for several hours at a time, but they do need interaction with their humans.

Because of their calm demeanor, some people have made the mistaken assumption that Persians are not very intelligent. Nothing could be farther from the truth. They are not a nosy or an inquisitive breed, but they do want the company of those they love.

Emotional and Physical Needs

Although many people do not consider these factors before they adopt a cat, you really must do more than feed and water these animals. They do have emotional needs, and Persians have definite physical needs.

If you are not prepared to spend time with your Persian, including the time that is required to groom their beautiful flowing coats on a daily basis, this is not the breed of cat for you.

Bringing Your Persian Home

Persians are very adaptable animals, doing well with other pets, including dogs, and tolerating well-behaved children with aplomb. That being said, however, they do like the major parts of their world to stay pretty much the same, which is a standard of the feline personality regardless of breed.

The transition from a cattery to your home is an important time in your kitten's life, and one that can be intimidating if not handled correctly. There are two areas in which you want to stay consistent: the litter box and the dinner plate.

Litter Box in Transition

Cats are incredibly particular about where they do their "business." Especially when you're dealing with a young animal that has just become accustomed to using a litter pan, you don't want to do anything to confuse the baby.

Talk to the breeder about the type of litter box the kitten has learned to use and get exactly the same kind of litter. If you are confining the kitten to a small area in the beginning, which I recommend, a single litter box is fine. As your cat gets more of the run of the house, two boxes is a better idea.

If, for whatever reason, you decide to change your cat's tray and litter, don't take up the old items until you know your pet is reliable and comfortable using the new arrangement.

Kitty's Dinner Table

For as much as cats are fussy about their litter boxes, they're even more attitudinal about what is put on their dinner plate. Since one activity has a direct effect on the other, you want to avoid gastrointestinal upset at all costs.

Discuss food choices with your breeder, and find out how the kitten would have been fed in the coming months if it had remained at the cattery. I like to remind people that cats are carnivores, so any food that does not list meat as the main ingredient is, in my eyes, suspect.

I'll talk about nutrition at length in the next chapter, but during the transitional phase from cattery to home, always give the kitten the food it's used to receiving.

Of course you'll want to have toys waiting for the new arrival. Make sure none of the items present a choking hazard and don't bother with catnip. Your kitten won't react to "kitty weed" until it has reached the age of 6-9 months.

Introductory Grooming

Grooming is also a topic I will discuss at length later in this chapter because with a Persian, you'll be doing a lot of it. By the time you bring your kitten home, the breeder should already have the baby accustomed to being brushed daily. DO NOT fall down on this routine!

Find out exactly what implements have been used and at what times of the day and under what conditions. If the cat is used to being brushed sitting on someone's lap, for instance, follow that routine.

You may actually want to ask the breeder for some grooming lessons, or inquire if you can come in and observe the entire grooming routine for an adult Persian. This is a vital part of husbandry for this breed. You want to learn how to handle the chore effectively and well, and establish a set daily schedule early in your relationship with your pet.

Also, be prepared for the fact that your cat will periodically require the services of a professional groomer. Persians are high-maintenance cats, and you aren't going to be able to do everything that is needed at home.

Let the Breeder Guide You

By this point in my comments on transitioning a kitten, it should be clear to you that I believe you should be guided in the beginning by the breeder's recommendations even if you fancy yourself to be an old hand with cats.

You have to remember that the breeder doesn't just know Persians, he or she also knows the individual kitten you will be caring for. The breeder will likely suggest some things like:

- Keeping the baby segregated in a small quiet area for a few days especially if there are other pets in the house. Companion animals tend to do best together when they are given a chance to introduce themselves with a paw under the door and a lot of exploratory smelling.

- Ensure kitty feels secure and warm by providing a cardboard box lined with a blanket or a store-bought bed to cozy up in. As they can sleep for as much as sixteen hours a day, this is important!

- Keep necessary items close by, including the litter tray, clean water and a bowl of food.

- Supervising face-to-face meetings with existing pets, but not overreacting. Animals pick up on our emotions. Your pets will work out a pecking order, and even though Persians are calm by nature, they are still cats with claws — needle-sharp claws when you're talking about kittens.

- Older cats may be threatened by a new kitten. Allow the older cat to smell the kitten and should they fight, separate them immediately.

- Keep dogs on a lead initially. Don't you worry, cats and dogs do co-exist just fine.

Of course you want to intervene if necessary, but pecking orders have a way of forming on their own and sometimes it's the new kid on the block that's in charge!

- Although initially everyone is excited and will want to hold the new kitten, it is best to introduce one person at a time and limit picking up as it can be intimidating at first, until your new pet settles in.

- Let your kitten decide when the time is right to explore the rest of the house by leaving the door open, and make sure you pop in to say hello as often as you can in the early days.

- Don't bring your new kitten home and then go out to work the next day. Make sure you are able to be at home for the first couple of days at the very least. A weekend is best.

- Establish a sleeping routine by closing the door to her room. Otherwise she will be jumping on your bed or playing in the middle of the night. Don't give in if you hear crying or scratching and soon she will give up, and it will become a set routine.

After a week to 10 days the kitten should be completely adjusted to the transition and ready to venture into larger areas of your home, which means you will need to do some kitten proofing.

The Basics of Kitten Proofing

If you just read that header and thought, "Why would I need to kitten proof?" you may not have ever lived with a kitten! They are a force of nature with which to be reckoned. Think two tons of curiosity that looks like a powder puff.

What I find so beguiling about kittens is that they have no concept of being small. Perhaps you've seen the poster of the tiny yellow kitten looking into a mirror and seeing a lion looking back? Nothing could be more accurate!

Get down on the floor at kitten level and have a look around. Try to put yourself in the mind of a pint-sized Persian on a mission to discover what's new in the world.

See that cord to the TV? Tape it to the baseboard. Do the same with every other electrical cord in the room. And for good measure, cap the outlets.

Not only are cords dangerous for your baby cat to chew on, they can also be used to pull down or tip over heavy and dangerous objects. At least in the beginning, I recommend removing all house plants from any area to which the kitten has access.

There are more plants that are toxic to cats than those that are not. I have personally instituted a "no plants allowed" policy in my home. If you do want to keep plants, research each one for potential toxicity.

Also, apply baby latches to any cabinet doors, especially those where any type of chemicals are being stored. Persians get less nosy and curious as they age, but kittens will definitely be kittens.

Keep small items that could be swallowed locked away, and definitely no plastic bags lying around. Keep the toilet lid down and the dishwasher and washing machine door closed at all times!

Learning to Converse in "Cat"

The degree to which a Persian uses its voice is completely dependent on the individual. I have had very chatty Persians, and others who barely ever uttered a peep.

There really is no single cat language we can understand, although the animals themselves have a very complex means of communication that involves facial expressions, body language, and smells, as well as vocalizations.

Over time, you and your cat will develop a language all your own. Experts say that cats understand 25-30 words, but can make more than 100 different sounds, whereas dogs understand 100 words and can only make 15 sounds. I read things like that and I find myself thinking, "Did they give the dogs and cats a vocabulary test?"

The real issue with comprehension and the whole "ignoring you" business is that a cat's hearing is geared for high-pitched sounds like a mouse squeaking behind the baseboard across the room. Cats ignore us when we're talking because a lot of human speech falls below the level of their acute hearing and must sound like a dull roar.

You can actually get a cat's attention far more quickly by whispering or hissing to him, and hand signals are often more effective than "commands." This may simply be a cat's native resistance to authority, but my Persians will completely ignore the word "down," but comply with a finger sternly pointed at the floor.

On the other hand, I've had plain old "alley cats," properly termed American Shorthairs, who could practically converse with me. One gray and white tom in particular had such an extensive vocabulary I would catch him responding to things I was saying to someone else over the telephone.

I have always believed that my cats and I communicate well because I talk to them all the time. This may make me a crazy cat lady, but I think the more you expose any animal to language, the more he will pick up — and the more you observe your cat, the more you will understand his language.

To get you started speaking "cat," here are a few things to watch for:

- Eyes that are wide open with small pupils indicate calm interest. Wide open with large pupils indicates fear. If the eyes are hard and intense, the cat is interested and focused.

- When a cat narrows his eyes, pulls his ears back and flat, and lashes his tail, surely even the most unintelligent human can get the message. "Back off!"

- Whiskers flat to the cheeks and ears out to the side indicate your cat is scared.

- Cats actually don't like direct eye contact.

- Walking with the tail flipped up and forward is a sign of good humor and relaxation. All is right with kitty's world!

- A yowl that runs through several octaves is called a caterwaul. You'll probably never hear this from a Persian, but this is the sound of a couple of tomcats fighting and it will literally raise the hair on the back of your neck.

- Chattering or teeth clacking is a personal favorite of mine, especially when it is accompanied by a kind of short little repetitive bark. Mine do this when they see a squirrel through the window. It means, "Wow! Would you look at that!"

And that ubiquitous "meow?" Adult cats actually don't meow to one another. That's a vocalization reserved for babies, which should give you a clear indication of what they think of us!

When your Persian rubs against your legs, he is marking you with its unique scent as well as enjoying the 'connection'.

The All-Important Litter Box

Cats are favorites as companion animals in part because they can live cleanly inside your home, tending to their elimination habits in a tray of sand or gravel. No need to take kitty for a walk. He wouldn't have any part of such nonsense anyway!

Litter Box Training

When you adopt a Persian kitten from a cattery where the animal has benefited from a program of socialization, the baby will come to you already litter box trained.

If you are put in a position, however, to introduce a kitten to its litter box for the first time, you will be shocked by the ease of the process.

Apart from beginning with a small litter pan sized for a kitten's smaller legs, you need do little more than show the baby the location of its "bathroom" at regular intervals in the day.

Gently place the kitten in the tray, take hold of its front paws and make scratching motions in the dirt. Cats are hard-wired to dig, do their business, and cover. Instinct will take over!

The best time for this training is once your kitten has awakened from a nap or immediately after a feed. Never punish if he doesn't use the box, but always praise when he does.

Potential Litter Box Problems

It is a source of both aggravation and sadness to me that so many cats are given up each year over litter box issues. If you don't understand anything at all about the feline psychology in the beginning, know that cats are clean animals.

If they go "off" their boxes, they're either doing so because something is physically wrong, like a urinary tract infection or a bladder blockage. The first thing any cat owner should do if their pet goes outside the box is get him to a vet to be evaluated.

Think about this from the perspective of the cat. You go in your box. You try to do your business. It hurts. So you try to find some place to use that doesn't hurt! The cat associates the pain with the location and is trying to get away from the discomfort.

As for poor box maintenance on your part, this one isn't hard to fathom. Think about an odor you truly dislike, something that offends all 5 million odor-sensitive receptors in your nose. Whatever it is, it's pretty disgusting, right? Okay. Your cat has 200 MILLION receptors. Imagine what a filthy litter box smells like to him!

Cats also have definite preferences about box types and litter textures. It's generally a bad idea to mix things up suddenly in either department.

If, for instance, you would prefer to use a covered litter box, leave the old open pan out and available until your cat has decided that the new bathroom is acceptable.

If you would prefer to use scoopable sand litter over old-fashioned gravel, transition slowly, mixing a little sand in with the gravel each time you clean the box, slowly increasing the amount until the box is filled with sand only. Remember, with cats, abrupt changes result in abrupt reactions.

Dealing with Accidents

If your Persian does go outside the box, you have to address the problem quickly, but not by disciplining your cat. You have some serious housecleaning to do.

The world of the cat is dominated by scents. Once a cat has urinated or defecated in a given location, his nose tells him that is now an acceptable place to relieve himself.

Accidents must be thoroughly cleaned up with a specialized enzymatic cleaner that removes all traces of the odor.

My favorite product of this type is the line of cleaners made by Nature's Miracle. They live up to their name and are quite affordable, selling in a price range of $5-$10/£3-£6.

Exploring Litter Options

For years, the only type of cat litter that was sold was made of clay-based gravel. This traditional choice is quite cheap. You can easily go out and buy 10 lbs. (4.53 kg) of traditional litter for $2.50-$5.00 (£2-£4).

The major problems with clay litters are the amount of dust they produce and their low ability to absorb urine. This leads to a lot of litter box odor, and puddles in the bottom of the box.

Since litter box trays are pretty much universally made of plastic, the more urine that puddles, the more often you will have to replace the box because the plastic has absorbed the ammonia odor.

Clumping Sand Litters

Clumping sand is an excellent choice for use with Persians because of its soft texture, and its lower ability to cling to the long fur on their paws and legs.

I will be honest, it's almost impossible to stop all litter tracking in the house, but I have found that sand is better in this regard than gravel.

You can buy a number of formulas including multiple cat, odor control, and low dust — and sometimes you can get all three in one. If you use sand, and if your cat is agreeable, I would recommend a covered litter box since a vigorous scratcher can send plumes of this stuff out of the box and onto the floor.

Also, be very careful and do not flush a clumping litter unless the word "flushable" is prominently displayed on the box. A clumping litter will quickly turn to concrete in the pipes. I knew someone who did this and they essentially destroyed the plumbing in their bathroom.

It is true that clumping litters cost more, but they offer a higher value in terms of efficiency, absorbency, and odor control. Mainstream brands that are readily available in markets and grocery stores sell for $18 / £12 for 42 lbs. (19 kg).

Eco-Friendly Litters

Eco-friendly litters are primarily made of plant-based materials and are meant to be biodegradable. The concept is great, but I have had great difficulty getting my cats to use them.

The problem, especially when these litters are used with Persians, is that they are so lightweight they cling to the cat's fur. Not only does that annoy the cat, but you'll be picking the stuff up all over the house.

As an example of an eco-friendly litter, you can get 20 lbs. (9.07 kg) of pine litter for about $10 / £7.

Absorbent Gel Crystals

Absorbent crystals made of biodegradable amorphous silica gel are a recent innovation in litter products for cats. They claim to inhibit bacterial growth and to prevent puddles of urine by absorbing and trapping the liquid.

I haven't actually tried this type of product, but I have cat-loving friends who say that the texture resembles that of gravel, which many cats enjoy, and the absorbency is superior to clumping litters. On average, you will pay $16 / £11 for 8 lbs.

Litter Box Design

Your basic choices in litter box types are the old-fashioned open pan, a covered box, and an electric self-scooping box. The old-fashioned pan is the cheapest, selling for around $6-$10 / £4-£6. The obvious disadvantages are the unsightliness of the arrangement and the scattering of the litter when the cat digs and covers.

If you have a cat that will only use an open box, you will have to cope with these issues by getting the box out of sight and putting down something to catch the litter debris.

Covered litter boxes are neater and many cats prefer the sense of privacy the lid conveys. I like the fact that the lids of the boxes are vented and include a filter that traps dust and helps cut down on odor.

These litter boxes come in a variety of shapes, from round to triangular to fit in corners. Depending on the shape and the size, covered boxes run $30-$50 / £20-£33.

Self-scooping boxes are a great idea, and work very well. I bought one as soon as they came out and got a mixed reception from my cats.

The idea is that the cat triggers a motion sensor upon leaving the box, thus activating a rake or a similar mechanism that removes the used litter (clumping) and dumps it into a receptacle. When the bin is full, you empty it or discard the entire thing.

One of my cats was utterly fascinated and would gallop in to watch the box every time someone else had to go. This created a bit of an issue with my older female who demanded complete privacy in the box.

My youngest male was absolutely traumatized by the "monster" and would have no part of it. Fortunately, I had plenty of other "normal" boxes he could use.

If you plan on using an automatic box, I would recommend introducing it to your cat as early in life as possible. You will pay $150–$200 (£98–£130) for one of these units.

Tidy Cats Breeze Litter Box System

If you have the budget for it, I highly recommend the Tidy Cats Breeze Litter Box System which retails for about $30. This gets you one litter box, one scoop, one bag of pellets and four pads. You obviously have to factor in the ongoing cost of the unique pellets.

The advantage in this system is that odors are greatly reduced because the hard clay pellets do not absorb moisture. So instead, the urine drains straight down through a grid to the pad (in its own slide-out drawer), leaving the solid waste on top to be easily scooped away.

Play and Interaction

For as playful as Persians can be, they do not have a reputation for being the great athletes of the cat world, nor are they going to tear up the agility ring in competition at cat shows.

I would describe the average Persian's approach to play as gentle and soft, preferably with a human on the other end of the toy. It's really the interaction with you that these sweet cats enjoy.

The rest of the time, they really are quite happy on the couch or placidly gazing out the window. One of the reasons the breed is so beloved is that they are calm and incredibly pleasant to have in the household.

As a species, cats don't have a dog's natural desire to please the "leader of the pack." Cats are more solitary by nature, and frankly more calculating. If they don't see a reason for doing something, they won't do it.

As cats go, Persians are more likely to do something to make you happy than many other breeds. They don't tend to try to make their humans march to their tune, but they are capable of being quite stubborn at times.

I am actually not an advocate of presenting any cat with a roster of "tricks," and then trying to force the animal to conform. In my experience it rarely goes well. Instead, I prefer to get to know my cats and create little private games that conform to the individual's interests and tastes.

I have had cats that could skillfully use their paws to turn door handles and one that loved to play a version of the "shell game." You know? Put a small object in one of three over-turned cups, mix them up, and you try to pick which one has the pebble.

This cat was highly adept at opening boxes and he loved tiny flat toys he could swat around on my hardwood floors. I would show him the toy, turn around and drop it in one of three boxes, mix them up, and then step back.

He would invariably walk straight to the correct box and extract his toy. This would go on for about 15 minutes, which is a cat's average attention span for a game, and then he'd go off for his nap, happy as you please.

With all "training" the key is to reward positive behavior. With a Persian, the greatest reward is always time with you, and lots of love and attention. They really are just furry lumps of love.

The games and tricks will naturally evolve if you just spend time with your cat, loving it and getting to know how it views and interacts with its world.

Ensure safety by avoiding toys with small parts that may come off and be dangerous when swallowed. A ball too large to fit into his mouth is a popular one, as are those fishing rods with a furry mouse on the end.

An alternative to buying toys are common items such as cardboard boxes, because your cat loves to play hide and seek. Try grabbing a tape measure and dragging it along the floor and just watch your Persian paw at it as if it was stalking and hunting prey.

Play is important because a bored Persian can lead to destructive and unwanted behavior.

Be careful how you use your hands. With overexcitement your cat can bite or scratch, not realizing how much this can hurt. Rough playing should be discouraged especially by children.

Scratch, Scratch, Scratch!

Persians are not known for being destructive cats, even with their claws, but they still will want to scratch. This is not bad behavior, but rather the cat fulfilling an instinct to clean and sharpen its claws.

Immediately take your cat to its scratching post the moment it tries to scratch an object you wish to make 'off limits'. Put the cat's claws on the post and make a downwards motion so you show him exactly what to do.

Whatever item you are most worried about — put a scratching mat or post near to it and spray with Catnip spray to attract her to it.

A simple $30/£20 scratching pole is generally sufficient for a Persian. Of course, our regal pet won't mind in the least if you pay out $100–$300 (£65–£197) for an elaborate cat tree with perches, tunnels, ramps, and observation platforms.

If you do have an individual that is a problem scratcher, try spraying your furniture with either pennyroyal or orange essence. Although I have never found these substances to stain fabric, you will want to test them on a small, unobtrusive area first. Both mixtures sell for $12-$15 / £7.87-£9.84.

Fluffy will also dislike anything "tacky" under his paws. Double-sided adhesive strips are an excellent and affordable way to discourage scratching. They're priced at about $8-$10 / £5.25-£6.56 per package.

Chapter 7 - Nutrition for Your Persian

The idea that cats are finicky is not really true. They simply have likes and dislikes as we all do. I would likely starve before I could be compelled to choke down Brussels sprouts.

The real issue is that a cat won't eat what it can't smell, and Persians tend to have respiratory issues due to the flattened state of their faces. If your cat has stopped-up sinuses, you may well have to get some pretty smelly wet food to ensure that your pet is eating.

It is never a good idea to try to starve a cat into eating something he doesn't want. It won't work, and it is a very unhealthy and arguably cruel strategy.

If your cat suddenly stops eating something he's always taken readily and with gusto, you need to find out if something is wrong. That "something" might be a cold or upper respiratory infection, or it could be an infected tooth.

I once inherited my aunt's psychotic Himalayan (which is supposed to be a lovely breed, but Ming didn't get the message) and was confounded when she wouldn't eat the same food she'd been demanding for 12 years.

I took her to the vet only to find out that the poor thing had two abscessed teeth in need of pulling. No wonder she was ill tempered!

Concentrate on Top-Quality Foods

It may not seem like a helpful statement, but it is an honest one — do buy the best food you can afford.

Cats are obligate (strict) carnivores, meaning that they require nutrition in the form of animal-based proteins (meat/organs) and not from plant-based proteins (grains/vegetables).

Therefore the best foods list meat as the primary ingredient. Cheaper economy foods contain more grain-based fillers and provide lesser quality nutrition for your cat.

It can also be false economy because your cat will feel hungry when he is not getting the required nutrition. It passes through their system without having much effect. So you end up spending more, by feeding more frequently!

Good quality foods have both high protein and fat content, with only a small percentage of carbohydrate required for your Persian's diet (about 5%).

The inclusion of Taurine, Niacin and Vitamin A are excellent signs of a good food as is approved by AAFCO. This stands for Association of American Feed Control Officials. This non-profit organization sets standards for pet food in the USA.

Fish, such as tuna, also contains excellent nutrients but this should only be a small part of a balanced diet.

Serve Both Wet and Dry Food

Because cats thrive best on a well-balanced diet, I recommend feeding both wet and dry food. Do not eliminate wet food in the mistaken belief that it will cut down on your litter box chores.

Cats need wet food as a critical source of moisture, and feeding wet food is also instrumental in weight control.

Dry foods (known as kibble) are much higher in calories, and will pack the pounds on your already fairly sedentary Persian. These cats are just ornamental enough in their approach to life that they can quickly develop weight problems.

Managing weight is more difficult with a Persian because the accepted visual gauge doesn't work well given the density of their coats.

Typically, you look down at a cat's body from overhead to ensure that there is a slight indentation behind the ribs and before the hips. Persians, however, will need to be periodically weighed.

Depending on overall body size, a healthy Persian should weigh 7-12 lbs. / 3.18-5.44 kg.

Just be careful to check the ingredients of any dry food as some are excessively high in carbohydrates, which isn't doing your cat an awful lot of good, to be honest.

The positive with dry food however, is that it can help clean the teeth, leading to less dental decay.

Try growing some cat grass in a pot. The folic acid helps prevent anaemia.

No Human Food!

Again, begging behavior in Persians varies by individual. The answer to stopping this problem is to never let it get started in the first place. Once a cat develops a taste for any kind of human food, they can be incredibly persistent about seeking the object of their desire.

Obese cats are at a greater risk of developing a number of health problems including arthritis and diabetes. Persians have big bones and are prone to hip dysplasia anyway, so you don't want to court problems by letting your cat become a junk food junkie.

Weight control is an important part of preventive health care for your cat, and something that is completely within your control!

Feeding Schedules: Kittens and Adults

Unless I have a cat with a weight problem, I don't make a science out of measuring portions. Kittens burn up a tremendous amount of energy, so I typically allow babies to "free feed."

Kittens are rapidly growing in their first year and need much more extra protein than adult cats. This helps them develop their tissues and muscles. Extra fat for fatty acids and plenty of calories are important in this stage of life.

Free feeding is the practice of leaving dry food out for your cat at all times, although having tried to measure this, I would say she consumes roughly 5 ounces of food each day (141 grams).

As the cat comes closer to one year of age, I modify that strategy, putting out half a cup of dry food per cat a day, which is roughly 118 grams.

When that is gone, I don't refill the bowl, but I do feed my cats a portion of wet food in the morning and again in the evening. An adult serving is 5.5 ounces (155 grams) per cat.

Many Foods Are Toxic to Cats

Beyond the obvious reasons for not allowing your cat to eat human food, there are many items that are perfectly benign to us, but dangerous for cats. Never give your pet:

- alcohol in any form, including beer
- grapes or raisins
- onions or chives
- eggs
- avocados
- yeast dough

Cats are often tempted to take a slurp of our morning coffee, especially if it's full of sugar and cream. Don't let this happen, and don't let your cat get into chocolate under any circumstances.

The caffeine in both of these substances can be deadly, and cacao seeds, from which chocolate is made, include substances called methylxanthines. These same chemicals are also present in most sodas.

Methylxanthine exposure can cause life-threatening symptoms in cats, including:
- Excessive thirst and dehydration
- Vomiting and diarrhea
- Heart palpitations and arrhythmia
- Seizures and tremors

Artificial sweeteners pose the same danger, especially those that contain xylitol, which has been linked to liver failure in cats.

Cats and Milk, Not What You Think

Of all the old assumptions that I try to combat in new cat owners, the idea that your pet needs a dish of milk or cream is high on the list.

Certainly your Persian will lap this stuff up if presented with the dish, but that's not the same as a need to be fulfilled. Cow's milk really isn't good for cats and can, in fact, be harmful.

If you know someone who is lactose intolerant then you understand that this particular sensitivity leads to extreme and painful gastrointestinal upset. The problem is created by the body's inability to produce sufficient amounts of the enzyme lactase.

Most cats don't produce enough lactase either! That's right. The animal most associated with a dish of cream is likely lactose intolerant.

Every species of mammal on the planet produces milk that is designed to fill the nutritional needs of its own young. Adult cats do not require milk — especially not cows' milk — and may experience stomach upset from its consumption.

You can certainly offer your cat a dish of milk as a treat on rare occasions, but milk and milk products should not be a regular part of your pet's diet. If there are any signs of gastrointestinal upset after your cat consumes milk, including an especially smelly deposit in the litter box, discontinue the treat entirely.

Making Good Food Selections

Like many other aspects of sound feline husbandry, I recommend discussing the matter of food selection first with your breeder and then with your veterinarian.

One of my Persian toms was prone to bladder blockages as a young cat. This condition can be present in any cat, and since he was a rescue, I have no idea of knowing when he was neutered. If this surgery is performed too soon on young males, their urethras can be damaged.

We tried all the conventional medicines, and this cat was still getting life-threatening blockages. He had always refused wet food, but the prescription dry food specifically designed to help his condition was not stopping the episodes, and he was getting a bit tubby. I was at my wit's end until my vet talked to me about texture preference.

Texture Preference

Like most cat owners, I was aware of texture preference in cats peripherally, but I didn't realize how pronounced the reaction could be. This particular cat absolutely will not eat chunky canned food under any circumstances. He will take one sniff and walk away.

Present him with a plate of pate that has a good bit of gravy, and he will eat every bite. As soon as I found a canned food he would eat, the bladder blockages stopped.

As I have said before, cheaper foods are going to have a higher percentage of grain fillers, so you want to go with items — both wet and dry — that list meat as their primary ingredient.

But you also have to be sensitive to your cat's preferences, and adjust accordingly. This may not just be a matter of taste, but also one of smell and texture. I'm lucky in that living in a multi-cat situation, someone is always willing to eat the leftovers.

Whisker Stress

With Persians, you also have to be aware of the potential for whisker stress. Most Persians have fairly long whiskers, and due to their facial conformation, they have to reach rather deeply into a bowl to get their food.

Cats with whisker stress don't like the feeling of their whiskers dragging on the edge of the bowl. Remember that the whiskers, or vibrissae, are sensory organs. You'll know this is going on if your cat frequently takes food out of the bowl and drops it on the floor to eat it there.

Using a plate, or a special tray-like cat bowl, will improve your cat's nutritional intake and stop the messy deposits of food on the floor.

Until you find a high-quality food that your cat will eat reliably and sort out all of his individual preferences, don't buy any brand or type in bulk. Some cats will happily eat the same foods every day for life, others will demand variety. You have to learn to understand your own pet.

Cat "bowls" that are specifically designed to avoid whisker stress are more expensive, selling for $25/£16 as compared to regular food and water containers that retail for $5-$10 / £3-£7.

The Food Budget

Although pet owners would love to know going into a relationship what it will cost to care for an animal, some factors are just too varied to nail down. Food is one of them. Beyond the issue of preferences, there are just too many brands on the market.

Based purely on my own experience with my cats, I think it's fair to say you'll spend around $75 / £45 a month on wet and dry food combined. The wet food will take up roughly a third of that budget as it is always more expensive.

Alternative Diet Approaches

Many pet owners are interested in feeding their pets an alternative or natural diet. This is both a reaction to reported deaths from contaminated commercial foods and an awareness of the dangers of chemicals and additives in all types of processed products — including the ones we eat.

The diet most often mentioned in this regard is the raw diet, which is also widely used for dogs. Please understand,

I am not advocating or decrying this approach to feline nutrition.

I don't use the raw diet, but if you are interested in this program for your pet, it is imperative that you understand that a great deal more is involved than simply offering your cat uncooked meat.

Adherents of the raw diet believe that our companion animals will more naturally thrive if they eat as they would were they hunting for themselves. Since cats are carnivores, this means giving them food that replicates the nutritional content of a fresh carcass — including bones.

Most veterinarians and many cat breeders, myself included, balk right there. Bones not only create a serious choking hazard, they also can mean lacerations in the throat, stomach, and intestines. Feeding raw also raises the risk of salmonella poisoning.

If the raw diet is used, meticulous food handling and preparation in a spotless kitchen with equipment reserved specifically for the cat's food is required.

Only raw chicken and beef can be used. Pork must not be included, and all food that is not used in 2-3 days, even if refrigerated, must be thrown out. No food is ever to be put in the microwave.

If you are interested in feeding raw, the information I have given you is not sufficient to begin the program. You must learn the precise methods to prepare the food, what equipment you will need, and what foods to use in combination to provide the right combination of vitamins and minerals.

NEVER begin a raw feeding program or make any other major alteration in how you are feeding your pet — cat or dog — without first consulting with your veterinarian and/or breeder.

The Importance of Hydration

Hydration is a crucial component of good nutrition for felines. Your cat must have a constant supply of clean, fresh water. Their water container should be wiped out daily to prevent the build-up of bacteria.

Many cats will not drink adequate amounts of water from a stagnant dish, preferring to drink from a running stream of water only. After my experience with a male cat that endured repeated bladder blockages, I prefer to offer my cats drinking fountains instead of water bowls.

These units have come down in price considerably, and I like them because they include changeable filters. You shouldn't have to pay more than $30/£23 for a feline drinking fountain and I find they last at least two years.

Blue Lynx Himalayan
Photo Credit: Joan of KaristaKats

Chapter 8 - Grooming Your Persian

Persians are solid, healthy cats with sturdy frames and big bones. Their long, flowing coats require daily brushing, and should be kept clean and smooth.

Unlike many breeds, Persians do need to be bathed to prevent oil, grit, and dander from building up in their fur and to remove mats and tangles.

Many of these chores can be done at home, but realistically, your cat will need the periodic services of a professional groomer.

Temperament and Grooming

Most professional groomers will tell you that cats come in gradations of three basic temperaments:

- Shy. These cats are frightened by the grooming process and need constant and steady reassurance. They are not aggressive, but they may try very hard to get away.

- Compliant. These cats are completely onboard with grooming and in fact enjoy the process. They are very easy to handle and are in no way aggressive.

- Aggressive. These cats range from those that hiss and swat to the sort that literally lose their minds and cannot be groomed at home, requiring a light tranquilizer or actual sedation to be washed and clipped.

Once you determine where your cat fits on the spectrum, you can more accurately judge how often the services of a groomer should be used. The earlier a cat becomes accustomed to daily grooming, the better.

Tangles and Mats

Tangles and mats are pressing concerns. On a daily basis you should use a shedding comb to remove loose hair and minor mats and tangles. These combs have two sets of adjacent wire teeth with one set longer than the other.

I use a model made by Coastal Pet Safari that retails for less than $10 / £6.12.

Preventing matted hair is a major goal of your Persian's grooming routine. Mats block the flow of air to the skin resulting in itching and infection.

In general, I do not recommend that you try to remove mats from your pet's hair yourself. A cat's skin is very fragile and becomes even more so with age as the animal loses muscle mass.

If the mat is a minor one, use your fingers and work from the base to gently tease apart the hairs. Do NOT cut the mat out. Work with your fingers and a comb until the affected area is free again. For severe mats and tangles, take your cat to the groomer.

Claw Clipping

Before you bathe your cat or engage in any major grooming chores, I suggest you clip your cat's claws. Professional groomers refer to a cat's claws as its "weapons of mass destruction."

Place your Persian in your lap and pick up one front paw, gently applying pressure with your thumb just behind the toes. This will cause the claws to become extended so you can examine the nail. The curved claw tips are translucent which will allow you to see the vascular "quick" at the base, which will appear pink.

Be extremely careful not to clip into this area, which will be painful for your cat and cause excessive bleeding. Snip off only the sharp points. The dew claw on the side of the foot is the hardest to reach on most cats, but I've found Persians to be fairly compliant with claw clipping.

My rule is always to exercise "less restraint." I try to make my cats feel secure but not held down and trapped. When you become practiced at it, claw clipping goes very quickly, and the cat really doesn't have time to get upset about the whole business.

Invest in a small pair of clippers designed for use with pets. I like the kind that is designed like pliers. They give a much better grip and more accurate control. This type of nail trimmer sells for around $10 / £6.

The Tail Test

If you have never bathed a cat before, or if you have adopted an older rescue Persian and you don't know how the animal will react to the process, use the "tail test."

Before you try to bathe the cat, put is tail in the water. If the cat doesn't mind, you should be able to proceed without fear of too much upset. If the cat loses it, you know you have a problem on your hands.

Use the same method for blow drying. It's much better to start trying to work at the tail than to be holding a cat that panics at the sound of the blow dryer and tears you up with its claws trying to get away from the "cat eating monster."

Bathing

If you bathe your cat at home, make sure that you have everything you need on hand. You want lukewarm to slightly warm water.

You may be surprised at just how long it will take to get your Persian wet. Their coats are very thick. Make sure that no water gets in the ears, eyes, or nose. If your cat will allow it, use cotton balls in the ears to keep them dry.

Never pour water over the cat's face. You can clean your pet's face with a warm wash cloth, but don't use soap around a Persian's sensitive eyes.

Degreasing

Once your cat is thoroughly wet, there are two stages to bathing a long-haired cat: degreasing and shampooing.

There are many degreasing formulas on the market. Be sure that you are using one that is specifically formulated for pets. It's fine if the label says "dog and cat." The material is a paste-like gel and is used exactly as if it were shampoo.

On average you'll pay about $15 / £9.19 for 16 ounces / 454 grams.

Be sure to rinse the degreaser out thoroughly. Your Persian's fur, even when wet, should have a velvety feel after using this product.

Shampoo

Find a shampoo that is natural, scent-free and hypoallergenic. Most of these products are sold in 16 ounce / 454 gram bottles or larger and retail in a price range of $10-$15 / £6.12-£9.19.

Gently work the shampoo into the cat's fur, but don't scrub, Make sure that you over-rinse the coat since shampoo residue will only make the hair tangle more easily.

Drain all the water out of the sink or tub and run your hands through the cats fur with straight motions "wringing" as much of the water out as possible.

Next, you will want to swaddle the cat in a soft dry towel. Don't scrub at the fur. Use drying strokes that follow the natural course of the hair.

Blow Drying

This is generally the deal-breaker for home grooming. Do you have a cat that hates the vacuum cleaner? Well, the blow dryer isn't going to be his favorite device either.

If your cat will allow you to do so, blow the fur on the lowest setting possible, gently brushing or combine the hair straight as you work.

You may need help with the cat's belly and legs. Make sure that all areas are dry and combed straight and clean.

Clipping and Trimming

These are not chores that I am willing to perform at home for fear of injuring my cat. Typically a Persian's coat will need to be trimmed back on the belly and inside the legs to prevent matting. This shouldn't be done on any animal that will be exhibited in a show, but it's a great advantage for household pets.

If you live in a region with extreme summer heat, you may want to get a "lion cut" for your Persian, which is essentially shaving the body and leaving a "mane" on the head and "cuffs" on the feet. This is much more comfortable for the cat and gives you something of a break from shedding and brushing.

Eye Care

Due to the problem of draining eyes with Persians, you will need to clear away any staining on the face. In order to prevent a build-up, I use a soft cosmetic disc made of foam that I dip in warm water.

On a daily basis, I gently wipe the area around my cats' eyes to keep the fur clean and soft. If necessary, you can do the same thing for any nasal drainage.

Ear Care

At most, I use a bit of cotton dipped in warm water to softly swab out the ear flap and opening to the ear canal to keep this region free of debris. Never use a cotton swab in the ear canal as you can easily injure your pet.

If there is obvious black, tarry debris in the ear and a yeasty smell, your cat probably has ear mites and a trip to the vet is in order.

Finding a Professional Groomer

At least every 2-3 months you will want your Persian to be professionally groomed. This may be required more often if you are unable to work with your cat at home, beyond daily brushings.

Ideally, you will be able to find a groomer who will come to you. Most cats do not like to be taken out of their home environment and will be calmer in a place where everything is known to them and familiar.

If your breeder is local, ask for a reference for a good groomer. You can also make inquiries at your vet clinic or check the bulletin board there. Be sure that the groomer you choose has experience with Persians.

Visit the grooming facility first, and ask for a tour to get a sense of how your pet will be secured while on the premises and how the work areas are maintained.

Make sure that the groomer requires that all animals brought into the establishment are current with their vaccinations, and that precautions are taken to keep the cats strictly separated. Many feline diseases can be transmitted with nothing more than a nose tap.

The cost of grooming varies widely by company and by service performed, but on average, a grooming session costs about $50 / £30.

Cat Crate

If you do have to transport your cat to a groomer, make certain you have a secure cat crate with a good lock.

Whether soft or hard-sided, these travel boxes range from $25–$50 / £15–£30 depending on size.

Since a crate is also necessary when you take your pet to the vet, this is an essential purchase and an item you should always have on hand for use with your pet.

Bluepoint Himalayan
Photo Credit: Joan of KaristaKats

Chapter 9 - Your Persian Cat's Health

Through the years I've had many people tell me they wouldn't have a Persian because they suffer from too many health issues. That may or may not be the case depending on the quality of the cattery from which you obtain your pet.

Due to their flattened facial conformation, Persians can suffer from deformities of the eyes and nose, and chronic breathing problems. Like most genetic issues in animals — and people — these things are not as predictable as we might like.

Any breeder that tells you genetic issues have never surfaced in their cats isn't being honest. In my experience, however, the greatest numbers of genetic issues present in Persians are in kittens that were bred in kitten mills or by "backyard" breeders.

This second class of people is not doing anything "bad." They allowed their cat to have kittens and made those kittens available for adoption. The problem is that they have no real sense of the genetics on either side of the pairing, so random problems are more likely.

I would never tell anyone not to adopt a cat under such circumstances, but I do strongly recommend that you have the kitten evaluated by a veterinarian first. Also ask a lot of questions about the parents and try to get a sense of their health. Meet them if possible.

Spaying or Neutering

The first medical matter new cat owners face with their Persians, especially if you have adopted from a cattery, is to have the animal spayed or neutered.

Breeders require that this step be completed before they release the cat's final papers, and you will need to present written proof that the surgery has been performed.

Costs for the procedure vary widely from one vet clinic to the next. You can find low cost options for as little as $50 (£32). However, I recommend that you take this opportunity to find the veterinarian who will provide your Persian's health care for the long term.

Your kitten will come with some existing medical records, but spaying and neutering will be the first vet experience you have with your cat. The surgery should take place before the kitten is six months of age, which is especially crucial in males.

If performed too late in life, or incorrectly, neutering can damage a male cat's urethra and make him more prone to developing bladder blockages.

Routine Elements of Health Care

There is no more important pillar of solid health care for your pet than maintaining a good relationship with a knowledgeable and trustworthy veterinarian. It is preferable, of course, that the vet in question has experience treating Persians.

For this reason, I am strongly in favor of feline-only practices where they are available. This trend in veterinarian services has been growing over the past 25 years and is, I think, quite positive.

The clinics are not only much quieter, which the cats enjoy, but the vets do all of their continuing education specifically in the area of feline medicine.

Interviewing a Veterinarian

I am the kind of cat owner who wants to be able to have detailed discussion with my vet. My comfort zone is all about information. Whenever I am anxious or unsure about something, I research the topic.

Whenever one of my cats is sick, I want to be talked to in a straightforward, matter of fact way. I like to have my questions answered honestly, but with sensitivity to the fact that the animal in question is a member of my family about whom I care very much.

A vet may be highly competent, but if he or she doesn't have a good bedside manner with *me*, the fit won't be good. The cat isn't going to like the experience no matter what!

If you don't already have a veterinarian, either get a recommendation from your breeder, or look in the phone directory or online for clinics in your area.

Make an appointment with the ones that seem most appealing, making it clear that you are a new cat owner, you want to see the clinic and meet the vet, and you're perfectly happy to pay for a regular visit.

Veterinarians are very busy people. Don't presume that they will just sit down and visit with you for nothing. Always treat your vet like what he or she is: a medical professional.

Prepare your questions in advance, and don't overstay your welcome. Get the information you need, including a basic list of costs for routine health procedures. Only when you are satisfied that a clinic will work for you should you make an appointment to take your cat in.

Observe closely how the vet and the technicians work with your pet. They should be calm, firm, quiet, and efficient. Do not interfere with their handling of your pet unless asked. Vet techs know how to handle cats that are nervous and anxious in their environment.

After the vet, my major concern is always that the techs are up to par. These are the people who will be handling my cat the most, especially if it is necessary for the animal to stay at the clinic for a procedure.

The Matter of Vaccinations

In addition to tending to the initial spaying or neutering of your cat, you will also have to decide to continue with or forego vaccinations. This is, for many pet owners, a controversial matter.

I am not going to come down on either side of this debate as I see merit to both arguments. Vaccinating companion animals against contagious disease has been a tremendous boon to pet health care for decades, and at least in the matter of rabies, shots are mandated by law.

At the same time, however, I have seen good evidence to suggest that vaccinations can cause tumors at the site of the injection. This is a highly individual decision on the part of a cat owner and should only be made after careful research and in consultation with a qualified veterinarian.

When you adopt a Persian kitten from a cattery, the baby will likely have already received some of its vaccinations, so your decision will be whether or not to continue with that program with the required boosters.

The vaccinations typically administered for companion felines include:

A Combination Distemper Shot

The combo for distemper is typically timed to be administered when the kitten reaches six weeks of age. Boosters are then given every 3-4 weeks until the cat is 16 weeks old. A final booster is given at one year, and then three years for the remainder of the cat's life.

The provided protection includes:

- Panleukopenia (FPV or feline infectious enteritis)

- Rhinotracheitis (FVR, an upper respiratory / pulmonary infection)

- Calicivirus (causes respiratory infections)

Some vaccines also guard against Chlamydophilia, which causes conjunctivitis.

Feline Leukemia Vaccine

Kittens receive the feline leukemia vaccination when they are 2 months old, followed by a booster a month or so later. Annual boosters are then given for life.

It is hard to over-stress the highly infectious nature of feline leukemia. Nothing more than a nose tap is required for this deadly disease to be passed on.

Persians should be strictly indoor cats under all circumstances. I do believe that the feline leukemia virus is essential for any cat that lives even part of the time outdoors. The risk of coming into contact with feral cats is simply too great.

Rabies

Most local laws require that pet owners have their animals vaccinated against rabies and that proof of this compliance can be produced. Rabies injections typically cost around $40 (£26).

On-Going Preventive "Medicine"

Although it may be difficult for you to contemplate, your cat, regardless of breed, looks upon its own pain and ill health as a dangerous matter to be hidden. A sick or injured animal is immediately vulnerable to attack by larger animals.

Cats conceal their illnesses because instinct tells them to. Persians are even more prone to do this because they are so placid and calm by nature. It is perfectly possible for your pet to be extremely ill before you even realize anything is wrong.

Daily Handling as "Diagnosis"

All pets should be handled on a daily basis, but since Persians have such a high grooming profile, you will be in a daily position to "diagnosis" any irregularities in your cat's condition.

Do not, under any conditions, hold back your concern out of fear of being seen as an overly obsessed, crazy cat person. You will know your cat better than anyone else in the world.

If you think something is wrong, get your Persian to the vet. Always go with your gut when it comes to matters of your cat's health.

As a simple part of being a vigilant and attentive cat owner, you should be on the look-out for:

Anything different in the cat's weight or the feel of its body.

It's a little harder to detect weight changes in Persians due to their heavy coats, but you should be able to feel the ribs slightly through a firm fat pad.

Differences in your pet's ability to move around.

Persians are pretty sedentary and ornamental by nature, but pay attention to how your cat jumps up on the couch. Does he show any signs of discomfort when he gets back down? Is he walking strangely?

Any of these things might indicate muscle or joint issues, or even the presence of a growth of some type.

Runny eyes and nose.

The potential for one or both of these issues in Persians is enormous. Later in this chapter I'll talk about some of the malformations of the eyes and nose that are a potential in this breed.

Do not neglect discharge in either area when it appears. Even if your pet simply has a respiratory infection, the animal should be evaluated by the vet.

Ears that are hot, tender, and/or smelly.

All cats are subject to infestations of ear mites and subsequent infections. If your cat's ears are putting off a foul, yeasty order and you can see a lot of black tarry looking clumps in the ear canal, take your pet to the vet to get the correct topical ointment and to have a thorough ear cleaning.

Don't attempt to do this on your own. You can certainly wipe off the ear flap, but don't try to clean down in the ear canal as you could seriously injure the cat.

Yellowing of the teeth with or without pale gums.

A cat's gums should be healthy and pink in appearance, and their teeth should be free of plaque build-up and any yellow discoloration. Dental exams are absolutely essential for the health of your pet.

All breeds of cats are prone to developing cancers of the mouth and throat. Early detection of such lesions during a dental exam could save, or substantially lengthen your cat's life.

Other elements of your cat's physiology that you should be aware of include:

- How your pet is breathing. The respiration should be from the chest, not the belly.

- The presence of any kind of mass or growth.

- The development of abnormal litter box behavior. This often indicates a kidney or bladder infection rather than "bad" behavior.

Remember, if you detect a change, no matter how slight, in your cat's normal behavior it is always better to have the animal evaluated than to wait until the issue evolves into something more serious.

Worming

If you acquire your Persian from a cattery, the chances are exceedingly slim that the baby will have intestinal parasites or "worms." This is not a difficult condition to diagnose, however, as the parasites are clearly evident in the deposited feces.

Should you see worms in the litter box, take the kitten to a qualified veterinarian for a full examination. A stool sample will be required.

The vet will prescribe an oral deworming agent, with a second course of treatment typically recommended in 2-3 weeks to make sure all eggs have been eradicated.

Hairballs

If you have a cat, regardless of coat length or type, you will hear the inevitable hacking in the night signifying a hairball is coming up. I have only been blessed with one cat in 40 years who passed his hairballs rather than vomiting them.

Hairballs are a natural consequence of self-grooming and they are not a health hazard except in rare instances when they can result in a blockage.

Typically in these cases the animal stops eating, is taken to the vet for an evaluation, and an X-ray reveals the hairball. Surgery may be required to remove the mass.

The best thing you can do to help prevent hairballs is brush your cat! Since Persians require daily grooming anyway, they may actually be less prone to vomiting hairballs than short-haired cats whose owners aren't as attentive about dislodging loose hair from the coat.

Potential Genetic Conditions in Persians

Personally, I have had extremely good luck with my Persians in regard to their health. Some of my cats have suffered from over-production of tears, but this is largely a cosmetic matter handled through daily grooming to prevent matting and staining.

All of the following conditions are possible in Persians, however, and should be among the items you discuss with your breeder prior to an adoption.

Hypertrophic Cardiomyopathy

The genetic disorder hypertrophic cardiomyopathy (HCM) can show up in virtually any breed of cat. The disorder causes a thickening of the heart muscles that can only be found via an echocardiogram.

As the disease progresses, the fluid will accumulate in the cat's lungs and blood clots will form, eventually leading to heart failure.

There is no cure for HCM and there is no way to guarantee that it will not occur in any breed or line of cats.

Polycystic Kidney Disease (PKD)

Cats with Polycystic Kidney Disease (PKD) are born with cysts in their kidneys that grow as the cat ages, ultimately leading to kidney failure. The first signs of PKD appear between the ages of 3-10 years.

Symptoms can include weight loss, deterioration of the coat, poor appetite, extreme thirst, and excessive urination. Dehydration will be present with pale gums, cold breath, and ulcers in the mouth. The kidneys will also be enlarged.

PKD can only be managed, not cured. Supportive treatments like special diets, the administration of subcutaneous fluids, hormone therapy, and the use of antacids can all help your pet to enjoy a better quality of life. The cat may live a matter of months, or do quite well for years.

Idiopathic Facial Dermatitis

The chronic skin disease idiopathic facial dermatitis causes lesions that become progressively severe over time. It typically becomes evident at about 2 years of age.

Black discharge will be evident around the eyes and nose, with redness, swelling, inflammation of the ears, and self-trauma from scratching.

The condition can only be managed and tends to resist any long-term solution. Usually corticosteroids are the first line of treatment, followed by cyclosporine. Medication will be required for life.

Entropion

Cats suffering from entropion have eyelids that curl inward causing irritation and damage to the cornea and potential blockage of the tear ducts. The condition can affect the upper or lower eyelids in one or both eyes.

The condition is often due to a congenital malformation like excessive skin folds, but can be the result of trauma. It is typically detected by redness in the eyes, excessive tearing, and squinting.

If excessive tearing is the only problem, no treatment is required, but if corneal ulcers have developed, surgery will be needed to remove the excess folds of the eyelids.

With appropriate treatment, the prognosis for complete resolution is excellent.

Blocked Tear Ducts

A cat's tear ducts will most commonly block after becoming inflamed or scarred. The most evident sign is excessive tearing. The condition is typically managed by keeping the area clean and dry.

Occasionally the ducts may need to be flushed in an effort to clear the blockage, but this requires heavy sedation and should only be undertaken with careful consideration.

Blocked ducts are rarely cured, but the condition is manageable and does not cause discomfort to the cat. The issue is more one of diligent maintenance for the owner.

Dental Disorders

Persians can develop dental problems due to the flatness of their face and the shortness of their jaws. Kittens are sometimes born with teeth that are poorly positioned and crowded, creating an environment ripe for the accumulation of plaque and bacteria leading to periodontal disease.

In pronounced cases, the teeth may protrude into the lips or opposite gum, causing abnormal wear, trauma, or difficulty chewing.

Signs of dental problems include, but are not limited to, bad breath, bleeding gums, cocking of the head while eating, chewing on one side, or an inability to keep food in the mouth.

Typically genetic tooth malformations become apparent by 14-24 weeks of age as the permanent teeth come in.

Professional dental cleaning is typically required along with special diets, oral rinses, and often the removal or shortening of some of the teeth.

Typically, the prognosis is good if the malformation is detected and treated early in the cat's life.

While vets recommend brushing their teeth on a regular basis, it has to be admitted that very few owners will do this — or even be able to!

One option is dental treats, my preferred brands being the Petrodex Dental Treats and C.E.T. Chews.

Giving Medicine & Recovery

Your Persian will want peace and quiet to heal. Stroking and petting may be unwelcome. Rest in a comfortable bed away from the noise of the rest of the house is best. A hot water bottle wrapped in a towel is soothing.

Make sure water and the litter tray are close. Food is better warmed up with small, regular portions good for recovery.

Try hiding any pills in a ball of meat, otherwise he won't eat it. Failing this attempt, then wrap your cat in a towel, so he is less likely to wriggle out of your hands. Gently tilt head back and pry open the jaw. Place pill as far to the back to the throat as possible while closing the jaw. This should trigger swallowing. Gently massage the throat to make sure, and reward your cat.

Wry Mouth or Wry Bite

This condition is an asymmetrical deviation of the lower jaw on one side causing the teeth to strike the cat's lip or palate. The twisting or curving of the jaw is evident in the growing cat and the animal is typically incapable of closing its mouth.

The standard treatment involves removing or repositioning the teeth to achieve a comfortable bite that allows the animal to chew effectively.

As Your Persian Ages

Like all cats, Persians experience variations of fairly predictable changes in their senses and abilities as they age, especially after the age of ten.

Usually they will sleep more and eat less as they age. However, you can't expect all cats to grow old the same way, and many remain quite spry throughout their lives.

Diminished Senses

Older cats will develop the same deficits as aging humans in terms of their ability to see, hear, smell, and taste. Often these changes are in no way apparent to you in large part because cats are so adept at coping.

One of my elderly Persians went completely blind over the period of about a year. I didn't even realize it until I rearranged the living room furniture and the poor thing started banging into chair legs.

I rushed her to the vet and was shocked to discover that she had little if any vision left. Often blindness in older cats is caused by unregulated high blood pressure, but in her case cataracts were the culprit.

Often older cats will begin to eat less, which can cause dramatic weight loss fairly quickly. Cats won't eat anything they cannot smell, so if your senior cat's nose is no longer as sharp as it once was, you may need to tempt the cat with smellier options.

This is a slippery slope, however, as often foods with a high odor can also cause gastrointestinal upset. I often dribble a little juice from fresh tuna or sardines on my older cats' food when they seem disinterested in eating.

This is usually just enough added scent to rekindle their appetite. Slightly warming wet food also enhances the smell. If these strategies don't work, consult with your vet about safe appetite stimulants.

Also try to include antioxidants such as selenium and zinc in food.

Physical Changes

Older cats have less muscle mass, and will begin to appear leaner. This is often difficult to see through a Persian's thick coat, so be sure to feel your pet's body conformation regularly. If you can detect the animal's ribs, have the vet take a look at the cat. Excessive weight loss is dangerous in senior pets.

Be extra vigilant about combing and bathing. Persians need a lot of help in this department anyway, and as they get older, they can't groom as well due to loss of physical flexibility.

If arthritis is present, especially in the hindquarters, you may need to have the cat's "britches" shaved more closely to prevent accidental self-soiling in the litter box. If you must clean your cat's "private" areas, do so with a warm washcloth and plain, clean water.

Personality Changes

Look for subtle changes in personality and behavior that can indicate sickness or even unhappiness. For instance, an arthritic cat that can no longer reach his favorite sunning spot may need a ramp or "stair step" arrangement in order to enjoy his beloved sun puddle.

Persians are very mellow and subdued cats anyway, so don't be surprised if your pet sleeps even more with age. This is simply a natural slowing down and is not generally a symptom of actual illness, unless accompanied by changes in appetite.

Since cats do instinctively hide their pain, always take your senior cat in for a checkup if you are uneasy in any way about his behavior and overall demeanor. Extra vigilance with older cats is always called for. Use your judgment. No one knows your Persian better than you do.

End-of-Life Decisions

Part of responsible pet ownership is having the strength to make end-of-life decisions for your cat. Sadly, I have had to do this many times. It never gets easier. I can't presume to tell you how or when to part with a beloved companion, but I can tell you that I follow two guidelines in making the decision:

- Advice of my veterinarian, whom I trust implicitly
- Wishes of the cat

To a non-cat person, the second criteria may seem absurd, but if I have a cat that is continuing to enjoy his life, is eating, and behaving normally, but requires a treatment or a medication, euthanasia is not on the table as an option, regardless of the diagnosis.

I know my cats well enough to know when they are in pain and are not enjoying a good quality of life. I do not believe that I have ever been responsible for causing an animal to suffer.

If you have not had the experience of being with a pet in those last moments, please let me assure you that with the assistance of a kind and professional veterinarian, the process is completely dignified, as well as being fast and painless.

In every instance my vet and her staff have made certain that my pet and I are in a private, quiet room. I have never been rushed to say my good-byes, and I have always been allowed to hold and comfort the cat. The injection, once administered, stops the heart instantly.

While that information cannot stop your pain, I hope that knowledge will at least give you some comfort when the time comes, when you must help your beloved Persian transition from the life you have shared together.

I also want to say that absolutely no one should ever sit in judgment on the decisions you make for your pet. I have spent large amounts of money on treatments for my cats, but I did not have family obligations that prevented me from doing so.

Whatever factors influence your decision, so long as you are motivated by kindness and a sincere desire to make the best choice for your pet that you can in the larger context of your life, no one can ask more of you.

Four Darling Red Show Quality Persian Boys
Photo Credit: Pat of Cleokat Persians

Chapter 10 - Cat Shows and Breeding Explained

Since most people who breed Persians either exhibit them or are regular attendees at cat shows, I wanted to discuss these two topics together.

I did not show my cats, but I have spent a great deal of time at shows, and, obvious as it may be to say so, they are in no way like dog shows.

If you've spent any time watching the Westminster Dog Show on TV and think you have an idea what it's like to exhibit a cat, let me correct some of your mistaken notions.

Dogs like dog shows.

Cats, at best, tolerate cat shows.

Of the various types of cats that you could show, Persians are much more compliant with the process than most. This does not, however, negate the one major difference in showing the two species.

Dogs are often not crated during their shows, being quite happy on their leads, getting groomed and fluffed, or lying happily at their owner's feet.

Cats are crated all the time. They'll make a break for it in a heartbeat — and everyone dreads the alarm call of, "Loose cat!"

How Cat Shows Operate

Cat shows are, however, rather gala affairs. Since the animals are only removed from their cages for judging, exhibitors have a field day decorating their assigned area.

As you are strolling up and down the aisles admiring the cats and the elaborate displays, you may think that the whole business is very laid back and quiet. Actually, it's a frantic process punctuated by long periods of often abject boredom — a fact vendors of all retail things feline fully understand.

It's extremely easy to spend a lot of money at cat shows on just about everything but a cat. This is not an adoption venue, and not some place you want to try to use to negotiate a purchase from a cattery.

Entrants are judged according to formalized breed standards drawn up by the organization serving as the governing body for the show. Each organization may have slightly different rules, but the show standards are essentially uniform. The major organizations in the cat fancy are:

American Association of Cat Enthusiasts
American Cat Fanciers Association
The International Cat Association
Fédération Internationale Féline
World Cat Federation
Cat Fanciers Association
Feline Federation Europe

Australia Cat Federation

Understanding the Atmosphere

The primary rule of cat show etiquette is also the one you will find most frustrating. Do not touch a cat without the express permission — preferably by invitation of — the owner.

This rule is intended entirely for the protection of the cats and was formulated for a clear and verifiable reason. Many deadly cat diseases can by communicated by nothing more than a nose tap. If you touched one cat suffering from an illness, and then touched a second animal, your hands could be the vectors of transmission.

If you are invited to pet one of the cats, you are being paid a supreme compliment, one that will be delivered with a bottle of hand sanitizer. Don't be offended. Just use it. Remember, you're taking care of the cat.

You must also resist any urge to try to be of assistance if a cat escapes. The best thing you, as a bystander can do, is to simply freeze. If you see the animal, you can quietly indicate its presence, but don't try to catch the runaway on your own. You'll only add to the confusion and scare the cat more.

Do everything that you can to get out of the way. It's quite common for a competitor rushing to the show ring to yell, "Right of way." Do your part and move. They have only a brief amount of time to get to the judging area or they will be disqualified. This is not a matter of rudeness, but expediency.

Keep your eyes and ears open and learn from what's going on around you. This is especially true when you're in the vicinity of the show ring. You can gain a great deal of information on individual breeds by listening to the comments the judges make as they are evaluating each animal.

The Persian Breed Group Show Standard

Judging in cat shows is a complicated business requiring judges to learn intricate breed standards. The actual awarding of ribbons and trophies is based on the simple fact that the cats that most closely conform to the ideal standard receive the highest marks.

Ranking the cats, however, takes an experienced and practiced eye. To give you an idea of the difficulty of this process, I've reproduced The International Cat Association Persian Breed Group Show standard verbatim below.

The Exotic Shorthair (ES) is the short-hair equivalent of the Persian and Himalayan breeds and is differentiated from the Persian and Himalayan by coat length ONLY. It is accepted in ALL colors. Its plush, dense coat and similar type give the breed a teddy bear-like appearance.

The Himalayan (HI) is a man-made hybrid breed identical to the Persian, but distinguished by the points on the cats' extremities (the facial mask, feet, ears, and tail) which results in a Persian-type cat with the coloring and deep blue eyes of the Siamese-patterned cat. The Persian (PS) has a long coat, flowing all over the body with a dense undercoat giving the coat full volume. The ruff should be immense. All traditional, sepia and mink colors are accepted.

Head	35
Ears	5
Eyes	10
Chin	3
Nose	5
Profile	5
Neck	2
Body	35
Torso	10
Feet and Legs	5
Tail	5
Boning	10
Musculature	5
Coat/Color/Pattern	20
Length/Texture	10
Color/Pattern	10
Other	10
Condition	5
Balance	5

CATEGORIES:

PS: Traditional, Sepia, and Mink.
HI: Pointed.
ES: All.

DIVISIONS: All.

COLOR: All.

PERMISSIBLE OUTCROSSES: None.

HEAD:

Shape: Round, broad, smooth-domed, with great breadth. Should be medium to large in size and in proportion to body. Jaws broad and powerful with perfect tooth occlusion. Cheeks should be full and prominent. Overall sweet expression.

Ears: Small and round-tipped, not unduly open base. Set wide apart, fitting into contour of head.

Eyes: Large, round, and full. Set level and far apart giving a sweet expression to the face, eye color has equal importance to size and shape.

PS/ES: Deep brilliant eye color preferred which conforms to coat color.

HI: Deepest blue preferred, but light to medium blue is acceptable.

Chin: Strong, full, well-developed, fitting into the face.

Nose: Almost as broad as long with open nostrils. Muzzle should be short, broad and full.

Profile: Short, snub-nose, definite break directly between eyes. Forehead, nose and chin in straight line.

Neck: Short, thick, and well-muscled.

BODY:

Torso: Cobby, firm, well-rounded mid-section, in proportion. Medium to large in size. Back short and level. The chest is to be deep; equally massive across the shoulders and rump with a short, well-rounded abdomen and ribs

Legs: Large bones, well-developed and with firm musculature. In front view, the forelegs should be short and straight from breadth of chest adding to sturdy appearance, not to have a bull dog appearance. When viewed from the rear, the legs should be straight.

Feet: Round and large.

Tail: Short and straight. In proportion to body length.

Boning: Heavy, sturdy and in proportion.

Musculature: Firm and well-developed, not overly fat.

COAT/COLOR/PATTERN:

Length:

(PS/HI) Long all over the body. Full of life. Dense undercoat giving the coat full volume. Ruff should be immense. Seasonal variations in coat shall be recognized.

Length: (ES) Short, but slightly longer than other shorthairs. Soft, dense, plush; standing away from body. Seasonal variation in coat and density should be recognized.

Color): (PS/ES) As described in TICA Color Descriptions.

Color: (HI) Clear color preferred with subtle shading allowed. Allowance should be made for darker shaded areas on coats of mature cats. There must be a definite contrast between the body and point color. The points, comprising of the ears, legs, feet, tail, and mask, must show the basic color of the cat.

OTHER: Condition/Balance: Should reflect excellent health and robust power with good muscle tone, well-muscled, but not fat. All parts of the body should be in proportion to each other.

GENERAL DESCRIPTION: The ideal PS/HI/ES is a strong cat with excellent boning and musculature, a well-balanced cat, giving the impression of robust power. The face should be round with a sweet, pleasant expression and large, round expressive eyes. The cat should be well-balanced physically and temperamentally, gentle and amenable to handling.

ALLOWANCES: Consideration should be given to the fact that females will generally be smaller than males, but should be in proportion and balance for their size.

PENALIZE: Long or narrow head; long Roman nose; thin muzzle; mild overshot or undershot jaw; bite deformity. Missing canine teeth in whole adult cats.

Asymmetry: While nature never creates a perfectly symmetric structure, recognition should be given to any obviously asymmetric head structure, (i.e., crooked or off-center nose, mouth, etc.). Such asymmetry should be penalized according to severity. Ears that are large, pointed, slanting out from the head or set too close together. A narrow chest, or long back. Poor muscle tone. Poor coat condition. Slab flanks. Small or close-set eyes. Pale, weak eye color.

WITHHOLD ALL AWARDS (WW): Overall lack of merit. Lockets or buttons. Poor overall condition. Eye color other than blue in Himalayans.

DISQUALIFY (DQ): Kinked tail. Severe malocclusion or extremely asymmetric face structure; crossed, slanted or improperly focusing eyes. Severe overshot or undershot jaw.

Temperament must be unchallenging; any sign of definite challenge shall disqualify. The cat may exhibit fear, seek to flee, or generally complain aloud but may not threaten to harm. In accordance with Show Rules, ARTICLE SIXTEEN, the following shall be considered mandatory disqualifications: a cat that bites (216.9), a cat showing evidence of intent to deceive (216.10), adult whole male cats not having two descended testicles (216.11), cats with all or part of the tail missing , except as authorized by a Board approved standard (216.12.1), cats with more than five toes on each front foot and four toes on each back foot, unless proved the result of an injury or as authorized by a Board approved standard (216.12.2), visible or invisible tail faults if Board approved standard requires disqualification (216.12.4), crossed eyes if Board approved standard requires disqualification (216.12.5), total blindness (216.12.6), markedly smaller size, not in keeping with the breed (216.12.9), and depression of the sternum or unusually small diameter of the rib cage itself (216.12.11.1). See Show Rules, ARTICLE SIXTEEN for more comprehensive rules governing penalties and disqualifications.

Revised 05/01/04 Persian Breed Group Standard, 05/01/2004

Considering Becoming a Breeder?

Whole books can and have been written on the process of becoming a professional cat breeder. That isn't the purpose of this book, but I do want to put in my two cents worth.

Whenever someone suggests to me that they want to open a cattery as a profitable business, it's all that I can do to smother a laugh.

While it is true that purebred Persian kittens, or any other type for that matter command high prices, I assure you the money goes right back out the door as fast as it comes in.

The only reason to go into breeding cats is love of the breed and a desire to cultivate a genetic line that showcases that breed to its ultimate perfection.

The questions you should contemplate before you think about raising pedigreed cats have very little to do with making money and everything to do about spending money — and about altering your life in major ways.

Do You Have the Time?

Breeding cats is not a 9 to 5 job. I'm talking nights and weekends. Vacations are all but impossible if you don't have a good support staff, and your holidays will be disrupted.

No matter how carefully I planned, I swear one of my queens could only give birth on a major holiday. I promise you, the cats will be in charge of your schedule, and they don't consult with you when they decide to mix things up.

Can You Deal With the Pains?

Yes, there are pains. No matter how confident I was that a kitten of mine was going to a good home, every good-bye was still devastating to me. I wanted to keep each and every one of those precious babies. That part never got any easier.

There were also the losses, the kittens that were born too small, or contracted a respiratory infection they were too small to fight. If you raise cats, you will lose cats. That never gets easier either.

Can You Pay For It?

The expense doesn't just involve equipment, but also the foundation animals for your line, or the stud feeds if you can't afford to buy a breeding pair.

There's equipment, food, supplies, vet expenses — you might even find yourself having to add on to your home and to put a liability rider on your homeowner's insurance policy.

What Will the Neighbors Think?

Persians are very quiet, so it's not so much a matter of the cats making a lot of noise, but is your area zoned for running a home business?

Are you a member of a homeowner's association? What are the HOA rules and regulations? What permits and licenses will you require? What will you have to do to pass health inspections? Is parking an issue? Waste disposal?

This is a list that can and should be very, very long. You do, however, have to live in your home and neighbor "wars" are miserable.

What Will You Do If You Fail?

Normally, I'm the most optimistic of individuals. I never start anything with the expectation that I'm going to fail. However, when you start a cattery, your welfare isn't what's on the line. You are responsible for the well-being of your cats.

If you fail, can you keep them all? If not, where will they go? Never even contemplate breeding cats if you don't have an exit strategy that is focused entirely on their needs.

Summary Thoughts

While it sounds like I'm being completely negative about the prospect of running a cattery, my true goal is realism.

If you fully immerse yourself in the cat fancy, learn everything there is to know about running a breeding operation, do all your financial due diligence, and still decide to move forward? You're in for a rewarding, consuming, and thoroughly satisfying experience.

But the gold standard of your decision-making should be this: what is right for the cats? You can make your own choices. They can only deal with the circumstances in which you place them. Never forget that, and you'll never go wrong.

Afterword

Obviously in a book about Persian cats, I'm going to be a cheerleader for all things Persian. It's pretty easy when you're writing about well-mannered, agreeable, and placid cats.

Don't think, however, that Persians are just couch potatoes. They're also loyal, adoring, interactive pets and great fun when they get it in their mind to play.

Although a bit given to picking favorites, they make excellent family pets. They'll get along well with the dog, and like nicely behaved children. Rather than be aggressive with rowdy kids, your Persian will just disappear until the coast is clear.

Certainly keeping a Persian means you are facing daily coat maintenance, but as someone who has run a cattery with very little help, I can tell you there's something very comforting about brushing a purring cat. For me, the grooming was as much meditation as chore.

Not only are Persians beautiful, they are sturdy, big boned, and on a whole, quite hardy. It is true that they can be prone to over-production of tears and some respiratory issues, but if you get your cats from a reputable cattery, those problems are rarely more than cosmetic.

My original Persian, Ashe, came to me as a castaway. He had no papers, but I always thought he was a pedigreed prince at heart. He instilled in me a great love of his kind and will always be "first" in my heart.

I hope I've been successful in kindling your interest in Persians and to increase your appreciation for their unique beauty and charm.

If you choose to welcome a Persian into your life, you won't have a bounding bundle of energy rocketing through the house, but you will have a sweet, steady, adoring companion.

Peace and contentment seem to be the particular gifts of this breed. Persians are lovely inside and out, and truly deserve their status as one of the favorite of all companion cat breeds.

Frequently Asked Questions

While I strongly suggest that you read the entire text of this book to truly appreciate the Persian breed, and to understand the care these beautiful animals require, the following are some of the most frequently asked questions about Persians as pets.

What should I look for in selecting a Persian kitten?

Kittens offered for adoption should be 12 weeks of age or older. They should appear happy and interested, with only a little initial shyness. Their eyes, nose, and ears should all be clean and free of any discharge.

The fur should be shiny, soft, and completely intact with no bald patches. The body should not feel bony, but rather solid and healthy. Ask the breeder to gently pull back the baby's lips so you can see the gums, which should be pink.

What's the best way to find a good breeder?

I personally think that the best way to find a really good breeder is to attend cat shows. There, you can see the finest animals a cattery has to exhibit. While this is not a venue in which you can adopt a cat, it's a great place to look at cats and to collect business cards.

Are Persian kittens born with long hair?

Persian babies are much fluffier than short-haired kittens. They look like little powder puffs, but their hair is not as long as it will become as the baby matures.

Do Persians require any kind of special diet?

While it is certainly possible for a Persian to require a special diet due to some sort of health condition, the vast majority thrive on the same kind of balanced and varied diet that is appropriate for any companion feline. I discuss diet extensively in Chapter 7.

How much grooming is required for a Persian cat?

On a daily basis, you should spend 5-15 minutes combing and brushing your cat's hair to avoid matting and tangling. To really keep their coat in optimum condition, the animal will need to be bathed, most likely by a professional groomer. To learn more about caring for the Persian coat, refer to Chapter 8.

What equipment is needed for grooming?

The best implement for the Persian coat is a metal comb with alternating short and long teeth. Brushes can be used, but since they may contribute to, rather than solve, tangling and matting, only purchase a brush after consulting with your breeder or with a professional groomer.

At what age should I begin to groom my Persian daily?

The sooner a cat becomes familiar and comfortable with daily grooming, the better. If you buy your Persian from a reputable breeder, the baby will come to you already accustomed to being combed. Discuss the cat's existing routine with the breeder, and replicate that schedule exactly.

Also, it's always a good idea to begin and end a grooming session by concentrating on an area that feels extra good for kitty, like just below the chin. You always want your cat to associate grooming with a pleasant experience.

Will my Persian shed more at certain times of the year?

Long-haired cats like Persians shed more in the warmer months of the year. Starting in the spring and carrying through the summer, you will likely have to increase your daily combing time to stay ahead of the shedding and to keep the coat fee of mats and tangles.

What problems will I encounter if I'm lax in grooming my Persian?

When long-haired cats like Persians are not groomed daily, their fur becomes matted. The hair knots and tightens, pulling painfully against the skin so that the animal may react negatively when touched. Matted hair is also extremely unhealthy as it cuts off the free flow of air to the skin.

In extreme cases of matting, a professional groomer will have to shave the cat so its coat can grow in again. You should never try to cut out mats on your own. A cat's skin is very fragile. You could seriously injure your pet. In instances of severe matting, seek the services of a groomer.

Is there any difference in temperament and adaptability in a male or female Persian?

While the gender question is a standard one, it isn't a question that I regard as necessarily fair or accurate. All cats, regardless of gender, are individuals. They all have distinct personalities, and they all respond to their life experiences.

I have had many Persians of both genders. They are all lovely, well-mannered, sweet pets. I do think the females are just a little more independent, and that the males are a bit more given to being couch potatoes.

Is there a problem with male Persians spraying?

Spraying can happen with a male cat of any breed, but it is not an issue that I've ever had to deal with, even with my intact males.

In neutered males, spraying is highly unlikely for the simple reason that they are typically altered within the first six months of life. At that age, they're too young to have even contemplated the spraying behavior.

Many people do not realize that female cats can spray too, but again, this is extremely rare behavior. In my experience, cats that are happy, healthy, and well-cared for just don't spray. This is a stereotype that is unfairly applied to toms, and in my experience indicative of an unhappy or physically ill cat.

If spraying does occur, it is much more typical in a multi-cat household where issues of territoriality arise. Again, however, this is not an issue I've faced with my cats even when I've had 25 and more at one time.

Relevant Websites

Persian and Himalayan Cat Rescue
www.persiancats.org

Blue Persian Cat Society
www.bluepersiancatsociety.co.uk

White Persian Cat Club
www.whitepersiancatclub.co.uk

Cat Fancier's Association
Persian Breed Council
www.persianbc.org

The International Cat Association
www.tica.org

Fédération Internationale Féline
www.fifeweb.org

World Cat Federation
www.wcf-online.de

Cat Fanciers Association
www.cfainc.org

Feline Federation Europe
www.bavarian-cfa.de

Australia Cat Federation
www.acf.asn.au

American Association of Cat Enthusiasts
www.aaceinc.org

American Cat Fanciers Association
www.acfacat.com

Split Face Tortoiseshell Persian
Photo Credit: Pat of Cleokat Persians

Bonus Chapter 1 - Interview with a Champion Breeder

I hope you have enjoyed reading this guide on Persian cats and we are not quite finished yet. This extra section is an interview which I did with Jenny Nicholas, an expert breeder and major cat show winner who owns Gemkin Persians in the United Kingdom.

Jenny thanks for doing this interview, can you tell us who you are and where you are based?

My name is Jenny Nicholas. I breed and show Persian cats under the prefix of Gemkin Persians. We are based in Denbighshire, North Wales in the UK, and started this wonderful hobby over 25 years ago when a beautiful white Persian came into my life.

I wanted to interview you because it seems to me you have an interesting personal story to tell given your recent success showing your Persian cats.

Perhaps we could start by you telling us what achievements you have just accomplished?

We have been fortunate enough to breed many Champions, Grand Champions, Imperials and Olympian winners and best in show winners.

In 2012, we attended the Supreme Cat Show for the first time in several years with our white boy, "Starwind."

The Supreme Cat show is the feline equivalent of the world famous "Crufts Dog Show."

To our delight, Starwind went on to win Best Overall Persian and carried on to win Supreme Adult and then the ultimate accolade of Overall Supreme Exhibit of over 1,000 entries!!

We were absolutely thrilled as Starwind was giving us a whirlwind of a ride, having already won many Best in show wins prior to this, but this is the show everybody in the GCCF wants to win.

This gave him the title of Supreme Imperial Grand Champion Gemkin Starwind. He continued to progress that year and throughout 2013. We attended a very exciting show called the World Championship Cat show alongside the Suffolk and Norfolk Championship show, again Starwind triumphed, under the lovely Christina Dugdale who awarded him as her Best Cat, Best of Best at Both shows!

Starwind continued to do extremely well in 2013 and we decided to try the Supreme again to try and defend his title which I am delighted to say he achieved, and was the first entire cat to ever win the Supreme twice!

At his final show of 2013 he attended another well-known show in the south of England, The National Championship show, where he picked up his 10th Olympian certificate and again won National Cat of the Year!

In total to date, Starwind has 11 Overall Best in show wins, and 22 Best Persian in show awards. Our goal now is to try and win his final Olympian, just one more to go, if he achieves this in his next show, he will be the first Persian to achieve a Gold Olympian title and will be the highest-titled Persian in the GCCF United Kingdom.

At present his title is Supreme UK Olympian Silver Imperial Grand Champion Gemkin Starwind. We are extremely proud of his achievements.

As well as Starwind's awards, we have been very fortunate to see our Persians achieve high awards with neuters we have bred and also our kittens, and on more than one occasion have won Best Adult Persian, Best Persian Neuter and Best Persian Kitten in the same show!

Photo Credit: Robert Fox

I'm sure a lot of readers think there's lots of mystery behind these cat shows, but how did it start for you and when?

It all began with the love for the famous "James Bond" cat, a Chinchilla Persian, but when I saw my first white Persian I felt that was the cat for me. Chinchillas are actually white cats with silver tipping, I preferred the pure white cat. My prefix derived from my first white Persian, Gemma Moon, and when I decided to breed Persians, I felt these would be Gemma's kin, thus became "Gemkin."

I know a lot of readers of this book are just interested in owning a Persian and may not necessarily want to show their cats, but to anybody who is interested, is it an impossible dream or can anybody start to show?

Anybody can start up with this wonderful hobby, and we also have the "YES" scheme in the GCCF in the UK to encourage the younger exhibitors. It is possible to show with a pedigree or a non-pedigree cat, it is your choice.

I would recommend anybody who is interested to visit the GCCF site (www.gccfcats.org) where they will find all the information they need. I would also recommend you attend a show or two before making your choice, and if you do decide to go ahead, with a pedigree cat, choose a breeder who is prepared to mentor you and help and guide you at the start.

What really determines success at a cat show?

The exhibit needs to be in prime health and condition, and needs to be well-handled and preferably have a social and outgoing personality. Cats that do particularly well are those who enjoy being show-offs and love the attention they receive at the shows. For pedigree cats they must adhere to the standard of points again provided by the GCCF.

An outstanding Persian will do best when in full coat, prepared to perfection without any sign of staining whatsoever, in gleaming health, having a lovely cobby short body, medium in size, with good bone, a very sweet look, small rounded ears set low on the sides of the head, with large eyes and good-sized nostrils, and of course perfect dentition and a short bushy tail to finish.

The exhibitor needs to be prepared to be gracious in defeat and always remember to congratulate others. Showing Persians must be a daily labour of love, grooming, nutrition and general well-being, play being an important part of the day for their development, all are of paramount importance. Fail to prepare, prepare to fail.

Do you have any advice and tips for people interested in showing?

Visit at least one cat show, meet some of the breeders, who will be happy to help and answer your questions. Visit the GCCF website which also provides a list of shows and show rules and regulations, they will also help with any questions you may have in regard to filling in your show entry.

Coming away from the cat show aspect, why do you think people should choose the Persian breed over another breed of cat?

Persians are often depicted as having a grumpy frowning personality, but bred and socialised correctly, these beautiful glamorous cats are the most loving, gentlest of natures, that quickly become attached to their owners and will follow them around wherever they go in the house.

Unlike many other breeds of cats, Persians are extremely dependent on their owners for their daily care and attention. They can live quite happily in a smaller space, but given the freedom to outdoors, will always require a garden which is cat friendly as they are not street wise. Generally Persians are of a quiet disposition and although they like to have their mad moments, they like nothing better than to be sitting close to their owners.

What advice would you give to people who are looking to buy a Persian cat?

Ensure you choose a reputable breeder, who will have the kitten fully vaccinated, wormed and often with free 4 week insurance and registered. Word of mouth is often the best way to choose your kitten.

Do not be afraid to ask as many questions as you need to, any breeder worth their salt with be more than happy to answer these, in fact if the breeder isn't prepared to discuss these with you, they will probably not help you with your kitten once you are out of their door!

Reputable breeders will give you some instructions on the care of your kitten and its diet and may often have a waiting list for their kittens. The breeder should have an extensive knowledge of the breed. Many breeders will often ask you to sign a written agreement, read this carefully and ensure you will be able to adhere to this agreement before purchasing your kitten.

Please remember, do not visit more than one breeder/ rescue shelter in a day and breeders may ask you to use anti-bacterial wipes before touching the kittens.

If you are interested in a pet Persian, you may also want to consider approaching the Persian rescue centres who do an amazing job of rehoming Persians, and rely on volunteers and much needed donations.

There are many different variations of Persians, what types do you think people should be looking at, or does it really not matter?

There are many different colours of Persians and coat textures, colour is individual to the person, but if showing a Persian, you will need to consider carefully as every coat colour and type needs a different preparation. Be sure to look into this and discuss with a breeder, or a cat club who has more experience in the particular colour you have chosen, before making your final decision.

The price of Persians seems to vary quite dramatically, do you think there is a minimum amount, realistically, that people should be spending?

I believe there is no minimum and no maximum. If you are looking to start your own breeding, be prepared to pay up to three times more for a show/breeding cat, as often the breeder has invested a great deal of time and money into the lines you are wanting to purchase. Unscrupulous and unethical breeders will often charge the same as any reputable breeder and you cannot go by this alone, far more important to do your homework first.

What would you say are common mistakes that you have seen Persian owners make?

Persian kittens are extremely inviting with their adorable characteristic sweet look and fluffy coat, but a new owner needs to remember Persians grow, and their coats will grow considerably, requiring daily grooming and eyes will need daily cleansing.

There seems to be some debate over nutrition and feeding, what are your routines such as how often and what types of food do you feed your Persians?

Our own personal preference is a natural raw meat diet for our Persians, we personally feel our cats thrive on this diet and our show results speak for themselves.

Obviously grooming is another major aspect of owning a Persian, can you offer any tips, advice and perhaps some accessories that you wouldn't be without?

Our own personal favourite is the greyhound comb and I would never be without this. Secondly I would buy the best quality brush you can, avoiding the plastic and artificial bristles that cause static and pull at the hair.

Every Persian requires bathing, whether you choose to show or not as the coat will become greasy with time, the more you bath your new kitten, the easier it will be when the kitten is an adult.

I would suggest bathing your kitten monthly if not showing, but more frequently if being shown. Grease is what causes the hair to mat. A good quality shampoo is best, we do not use human shampoo as it does not have the correct PH balance for cats and some can be toxic for cats.

We always dry our Persians with our blaster dryer, but as long as the coat is thoroughly dried with a hair dryer, this will prevent mats.

Eye cleaning is essential as due to the large eye, they can be prone to debris and infection, and there are many good quality eye cleaners available now. Eye Envy, Page One, Anna and Breeder Care are all good quality eye cleaners, but it is equally important to dry underneath the eye thoroughly, and use either of these brands of eye powder below the eye line and the crease around the top of the nose to keep the surface dry and prevent staining, taking great care not to allow powder into the eyes or the nostrils.

Are there any final thoughts that you feel the readers of this book would benefit from?

My final thoughts would be to remember most Persians live between the ages of around 14 and 18 and please when choosing your kitten, ask yourself if you can commit to this.

If you are considering having a family, please think will you still want and love your Persian?

If you normally go for frequent holidays, do you have somebody in mind who can take good care of your Persian?

If you can say yes to these questions I wish you well with your new journey, of sharing the joy of this magnificent breed.

Showing Persian cats takes a huge amount of dedication but at the beginning of your show day, when your Persian is waiting there to be judged, looking magnificent, you will have an overwhelming sense of pride.

I would like to take this opportunity to thank my partner Christian for all his support in sharing this wonderful hobby and also to my three children Zara, Gareth and Kelly, for supporting and putting up with my obsession of Persian cats, I love you all very much.

Photo Credit: Jane Gregory

Thanks so much Jenny for sharing your expertise and just for sharing your unique story with everyone.

Bonus Chapter 2 - A Love of Cats

This second bonus chapter comes from Amber Lea Morgan of Rarebreed Cattery. I encouraged Amber to share her story when she revealed to me the story of her boys taking part in cat shows. I hope you agree with me that it was well worth sharing...

From the time I was a small child, I have always had a love affair with cats. It must have come from my father.

Our first family cat was a purebred, seal point, Siamese named Tiki that my father rescued. She was slender and long bodied, with fine boning and a very long, triangular shaped face.

My father had a special way with her that no one else had. He could pet her and hold her, but I could pet her head no more than three times in one sitting. Any more than those few pets and she would run me out of the room. When Tiki left us, the house seemed incredibly empty.

I remember the first cat that I brought home without my parents' help. She was a seal point Siamese mix with an apple-shaped head and a large, round body. She was strikingly different from Tiki, and I called her Samantha. I found her "abandoned" in the neighbor's yard, and quickly scooped her up to bring her home with me. You can only imagine my mother's face when she walked in to find her 5-year-old child holding the neighbor's cat hostage!

She quickly advised me that this lovely kitty was not lost, but just out for a walk, so of course I had to take her back and explain to the neighbors that she had been cat-napped against her will.

When our neighbors moved to a home that didn't allow pets they graciously gave Samantha to our family. The neighbors never told us that Samantha was not spayed, so of course we were surprised when she had her first litter of kittens the year after she came to us.

Samantha was an excellent mother, feeding and cleaning her kittens as a good mother should, and never asking for help. She let me touch and hold her babies from day one, and every day after school I raced home to cuddle each one.

When Samantha's litter was weaned and ready for homes we had Samantha spayed, and I convinced my mother to let me keep one of her female kittens. Now we were a two cat home, and our new seal point baby became known as Skidder.

Skidder and I had a very special bond. Skidder would walk me to school in the morning, and would wait in the tree nearby when school was out. When school was out we would then walk home and enjoy each other's company over homework.

When I married my husband and left my childhood home, Skidder stayed with my parents.

Two years after I left home my parents moved 12 hours away and they took Skidder with them. I was devastated, but through my grief I knew that it was time to start looking for a cat for my growing family.

By now I had a 2-year-old son, and I wanted him to have the same experience that I had with my cats while growing up. Through my cats I learned about friendship, compassion, and loyalty. I wanted my children to learn these same things.

I eventually visited an adoption fair at a local Petco and quickly fell in love with another seal point Siamese mix kitten. She came to us freshly spayed but never seemed to recover the way we expected her to. A trip to the vet 5 days later revealed that she had ringworm, respiratory infection, and an infected spay incision.

I was devastated when she did not survive treatment, but even more shocked to find that the group who rescued her and found her a home with us felt that this was normal. I knew that my next cat would need to come from a breeder who would give a health guarantee.

While looking at Siamese breeders on the Internet, I came across the Persian breed and, for the first time in my life, I decided that a breed other than the Siamese would be well suited for our family.

As much as I loved the Siamese, they were more slender in body than I preferred. They were also very active and loved to hunt prey. The Persians were round and heavy bodied

like the Siamese mixes that I had in my youth, and their
sweet purr-sonalities and low activity level appealed to me.

They were described as being very good with children,
which I felt was important now I had two small children in
my home, and were further described as not being great
hunters. What a perfect match for a busy mom with small
children.

The only drawback to the Persian was their long, high-
maintenance coat type. I read that weekly baths were
required and that I would have to brush the coat daily.
Those that didn't want to do this could shave the coat to a
lion-cut, which greatly changed the overall look of the
breed.

Being a mother with a busy schedule led me to believe that
I would not have time to maintain a longer coat, and I
certainly didn't want to shave a cat frequently, so I decided
to adopt a Persian with short hair rather than one with long
hair.

My search for a Shorthair Persian eventually led me to
discover the Exotic Shorthair, which is the breed name of
the Persian cats being bred for a shorter coat type. At first I
wanted a brown tabby with a classic pattern, but then I
came across the red tabby color with a classic pattern.

The red classic tabby reminded me a lot of Garfield, and I
was not surprised to learn that Garfield was first a Maine
Coon who became an Exotic Shorthair later in his cartoon

life. I knew that I had found my breed of cat and the color that I hoped to adopt. The decision had been made.

My first Exotic Shorthair was a red, classic tabby named Flame and I bought her from Anne Ritzinger of Ritz-O-Cats when she was 6 months old. My only intention was to purchase Flame as a well-loved pet for me and my children, but after sharing pictures of Flame with Anne, I discovered that I had accidentally bought a show cat.

I was quite surprised when Anne invited me to my first cat show. I had no idea how to show a cat, but Anne promised that she would help me to get ready.

I went to my first cat show with my then 3-year-old and 6-month-old sons, Gavin and Trent. We entered the raffle, winning the large cat tree, and Flame brought home several ribbons that I did not understand. Anne told me that many cats did not get ribbons in their first show.

That was all I needed to hear to decide to enter my second cat show. Something in me felt that Flame was special, and I wanted to share that with the world.

My children always came with me to the shows and quickly found ways to get into mischief while I was busy making sure that Flame was ready for each judging.

I will never forget the time that my sons played "jungle" in the flower beds outside of the show hall, crushing the flowers and requiring us to pay for their replacement, or the time they played in the water of the bathroom sinks until their clothes were soaking wet and the bathroom floor was a muddy mess.

The other exhibitors were not as amused as I was and made it very clear that this was a professional environment where naughty children were not tolerated.

I suppose that I could have hired a babysitter and left my two boys at home, but I found an alternate solution to their boredom by having them brush Flame and carry her up to each judging station when her number was called. Much to my surprise, my children enjoyed the experience and all of their mischievous moments dissipated.

Eventually we bred Flame and had our first litter of kittens. We also helped raise kittens for Anne while she was away at cat shows, and our family love of showing Flame turned into a love of raising and showing purebred cats. With each litter we were very careful in matching parents that would produce the best possible kittens, and soon we began keeping cats to show that would carry our cattery name.

With my two boys helping to raise, groom, and show our cats to top titles, I felt it was only fair that they be listed as the owners of our cats on registration paperwork. This also meant that every litter would also show them as the breeders of record.

They were now showing cats that they had worked hard to produce and were accepting titles and awards with their names on the certificates. They were learning all of the things I had hoped they would, which were friendship, compassion, and loyalty.

Eventually the major cat organizations created a forum for children to participate in, which was called Junior Showmanship. My kids eagerly joined the program, as they had been showing for years before the program was developed and loved all things cat and cat show related.

Through Junior Showmanship, my children developed public speaking skills by giving an oral presentation of their cat's strengths and weaknesses. They also described how a cat of our breed should look and behave, and exhibited projects that demonstrated their knowledge in showing, breeding, and their skill level.

My children soon found themselves winning Best Junior in Show, and their career in cats was truly coming full circle.

What started out as adopting a pet cat that mom owned and showed was now becoming a cattery managed and shown by my two elementary-aged children.

There is a deep sense of pride that is earned with every award your cat earns, but having your children earn these awards with their hard work and effort is something that words cannot describe.

Our cats were always raised in our home as members of our family, so each title earned and each award accepted was also a reflection on the love and care that we gave to our cats as valued family members. That, to me, is what cat showing should be about.

As I look back on the past 10 years, I have such fond memories of our cats and the shows they competed in.

These years have been amazing for me and my family, and I would encourage anyone with a love for cats to consider a career in showing.

Cat shows have opportunities for household pets (mixed breeds) to be shown, as well as purebred cats. They will even allow a cat to be spayed or neutered before being shown. With that in mind, there is something for everyone.

I would encourage you to visit a show and see if there is something for you.

By Amber Lea Morgan of Rarebreed Cattery

Glossary

A

Ailurophile — A lover of cats.

Ailurophobe — One who fears and/or hates cats.

Allergen — The primary allergen produced by cats to which sensitive individuals react is the protein Fel d 1 produced by the animals' sebaceous and salivary glands. Fel d 1 is especially spread in the environment by dried flakes of saliva on the fur from grooming.

Allergy — An individual exhibiting a high degree of sensitivity to a known irritant, as in the Fel d 1 in cats. The symptoms of the allergic reaction may include sneezing, itching and watering of the eyes, and skin rashes.

Alter — A term used in reference to the surgical procedures that render companion animals incapable of reproduction i.e. neutering or spaying.

B

Bloodline — A bloodline establishes an animal's pedigree by supplying a verifiable line of descent. Catteries carefully cultivate their animals' bloodlines in an effort to produce the highest possible exemplars of the given breed.

Breed Standard — Breed clubs and official feline organizations like The International Cat Association (TICA) formulate standards of excellence for breed to be used as a basis for evaluating the quality of the animals for breeding and showing purposes.

Breed — An animal is said to belong to a particular breed when it shares specifically defined physical characteristics derived from a common ancestry that "breed true" or are reliably passed on to subsequent generations.

Breeder — A breeder is an individual who works to produce superior examples of a given breed of cat (or other animal) through the carefully selected pairing of dams and sires. The principle purpose of breeding is to both maintain and improve the genetic quality of the breed in question.

Breeding — Breeding refers to the pairing of dams and sires in controlled reproductive programs for the express purpose of producing high quality offspring.

Breeding Program — A breeding program is a planned mating of carefully chosen dams and sires to cultivate ideal examples of a given breed.

Breeding Quality — An animal's breed quality describes the degree to which an individual conforms to the breed standard for subsequent purposes of showing or participation in a breeding program.

Breed True — When male and female cats of a given breed mate and produce offspring that possess the same traits, all conforming to the recognized standard for the breed, the line is said to "breed true."

C

Carpal Pads — A cat's carpal pads are located on the front legs at the region roughly correlating with the human wrist. Their purpose is to provide greater traction for the animal while walking.

Castrate — The surgical removal of a male cat's testicles to render him incapable of impregnating females.

Caterwaul — A shrill and discordant feline vocalization.

Cat Fancy — The "cat fancy" is an aggregate term to define all of the groups, associations, and clubs as well as their members that exist for the purpose of breeding and showing cats.

Catnip — Cat nip (Nepeta cataria) is a perennial herb containing high levels of an aromatic oil to which cats are strongly attracted. In response to exposure to "nip," cats display a kind of intoxication similar to what humans experience when they are "stoned." A cat must be older than 8-9 months of age to respond to catnip, and some individuals are completely immune to the herb's effects.

Cattery — A cattery is a facility where cats are kept for the purpose of breeding to promulgate a specific breed and bloodline.

Certified Pedigree — A certified pedigree is one that has been officially issued by a feline registering association.

Clowder — The collective term "clowder" refers to an assemblage or group of cats.

Coat — The overall term used in reference to a cat's fur.

Crate — A crate is a container used for the safe transport or temporary confinement of cats and other small companion animals.

Crepuscular — The correct term to describe the times at which cats are most active, dawn and dusk. Contrary to popular perception, cats are not nocturnal.

Crossbred — When a dam and sire of different breeds produce offspring, the kittens are said to be crossbred.

D

Dam — In a breeding pair of cats, the female is the dam. Also called a queen.

Dander — Dander is often responsible for the allergic reaction some sensitive people display in the presence of cats. The small scales are shed by the animal's hair and skin, and contain the Fel d 1 protein from the animal's saliva, transferred during self-grooming.

Declawing — Declawing is a surgical procedure to amputate the last digit of a cat's feet for the purpose of removing its claws. The operation is illegal in Europe, and also in many parts of the United States. Declawing is highly controversial and generally considered to be inhumane and cruel.

Desex — Desexing is the alteration of an animal by neutering or spaying to render the individual incapable of reproduction.

Domesticated — Animals that live and/or work tamely with humans whether by training or choice are said to be domesticated.

E

Ear Mites — Ear mites are microscopic parasites that cause extreme itching and discomfort by feeding on the lining of a cat's ear canal. Their presence generates a strong, foul odor and causes a build-up of black, tarry debris.

Entire — A cat is said to be "entire" when the individual is in possession of its complete reproductive system.

Exhibitor — An individual who participates in an organized cat show competitively with his or her animal or animals is an exhibitor.

F

Fel d 1 — The Fel d 1 protein is produced by a cat's sebaceous glands and is also present in the animal's saliva. This is the substance that triggers an adverse allergic reaction in some sensitive people.

Feline — Felines are members of the family *Felidae*, which includes lions, tigers, jaguars, and both wild and domestic cats.

Fleas — Fleas are wingless, bloodsucking insects in the order *Siphonaptera* that feed off warm-blooded animals, causing scratching and skin irritation, and in severe cases, anemia.

Flehmening/Flehmen Reaction — The Flehmen Reaction is a facial gesture in cats often mistaken for a grimace. When a cat partially opens its mouth and curls back its upper lip, the animal is drawing air over two special openings in the roof of the mouth just behind the front teeth. These second "nostrils" allow a cat to "taste" what it smells.

G

Gene pool — In any population of organisms, the "gene pool" is the group's collective genetic information.

Genes — Genes are the distinct hereditary units consisting of a DNA sequence that occupies a specific location on a chromosome. Genes determine the particular physical characteristics of an organism.

Genetic — Any trait, characteristic, tendency, or condition that is inherited is said to be genetic in nature.

Genetically Linked Defects — Specific health conditions or other perceived flaws that are passed from one generation to the next are considered to be genetically linked defects.

Genetics — Genetics is the scientific study of heredity.

Genotype — The genetic makeup of an organism or a group of organisms is called the genotype.

Grooming — The necessary procedures to care for the coat of a feline are called grooming and typically include brushing, combing, trimming, or washing.

H

Heat — When a female mammal such as a cat enters her seasonal estrus cycle the phase is colloquially referred to as "going into heat."

Hereditary — Characteristics, traits, diseases, or conditions genetically transmitted from parent to offspring are said to be hereditary.

Histamine — A physiologically active amine released by mast cells in plant and animal tissue as part of an allergic reaction.

Hock — The anatomical term for that part of a cat's hind leg that is the rough equivalent of the human ankle.

Household Pet — Unlike dog shows, cat shows have a division for "household pets," which are non-pedigreed individuals. This competition is extremely popular with young people and a starting ground for many new enthusiasts in the cat fancy.

Housetraining — The process of teaching an animal to live cleanly in a house using a box of sand or gavel litter for urination and defecation is called "housebreaking."

I

Immunization — Immunizations, also called inoculations or vaccinations, are injections intended to create immunity against disease.

Innate — Qualities, traits, and tendencies that are present at birth and therefore, inborn, are said to be innate.

Inbreeding — The mating of two closely-related cats is said to be inbreeding, and is typically the cause of genetic defects.

Instinct — Inborn patterns of behavior in a species that are triggered by specific environmental stimuli are called "instincts."

Intact — Animals that have not been spayed or neutered and that are in possession of their complete reproductive system are said to be intact.

J

Jacobsen's Organ — This is a highly specialized organ in the roof of a cat's mouth. Two extra "nostrils" located just behind the upper front teeth allow the cat to "taste" a scent when air passes over the openings.

K

Kindle — Like "clowder," a "kindle" is a collective term for a group of cats, but in this instance refers specifically to kittens.

Kitten — A kitten is a cat of less than 6 months of age.

L

Lactation — The formation and secretion of milk by the mammary glands for the nourishment of young mammals.

Lactating — When a mammalian mother is producing milk for her offspring, she is said to be lactating.

Litter — Felines give birth to 3-4 kittens on average, with 6-10 possible. These multiple offspring groups are referred to as litters.

Litter Box — A litter box is a container holding sand or clay that allows a cat to live cleanly in the house by providing the animal with an acceptable place to urinate and defecate.

Long-haired – Long-haired cats are any breed, like a Persian, that have coats made up of varying lengths of long hair. These same animals usually also display prominent neck ruffs and plumed tails.

M

Mites — Tiny parasites from the order *Acarina* are called mites. They infest both plants and animals, and are often present in the ear canals of domestic cats.

Muzzle — That part of the head and face of a cat that projects forward. This region includes the mouth, nose, and jaws, and may also be referred to as the snout.

N

Neuter — A term used to describe the surgery for castrating a male cat to prevent him from impregnating a female.

Nictitating Membrane — The nictitating membrane is the transparent inner or "third" eyelid on cats that protects and moistens the eye.

Nocturnal — Animals that are nocturnal are most active at night. This term is used in error with cats as these creatures are most active at dusk and dawn, and are therefore crepuscular.

O

Odd-Eyed — In odd-eyed cats, each eye is a different color.

P

Papers — The colloquial term for the official documentation of a cat's pedigree and registration is "papers."

Pedigree — A pedigree is the written verifiable ancestry of a cat of a particular breed spanning three or more generations.

Pet Quality — A pet quality pedigreed cat is one that fails to sufficiently conform to the standard for the breed to be used in a breeding program or to be exhibited for competition.

Q

Queen — Queens are intact female cats in possession of their complete reproductive system.

Quick — The "quick" of a cat's claw is the vascular portion at the base that will bleed profusely if accidentally clipped.

R

Rabies — Rabies is a highly infectious viral disease fatal in warm-blooded animals. It is transmitted by the bite of an infected animal and attacks the victim's central nervous system.

Registered Cat — A registered cat is one that has been documented via a recognized feline association in regard to its breed and pedigree.

Registered Name — A cat's registered name is the name used to verify its breed and pedigree. Such names are typically long, and made up of some combination of the names of the cat's sire and dam.

S

Scratching Post — Any structure covered in carpet or rope and designed to be used by a cat to sharpen and clean its claws without being destructive to household furnishings is referred to as a scratching "post."

Show — Cat shows are organized exhibition where cats are judged competitively for the degree to which they conform to accepted breed standards.

Show Quality — Show quality cats in any breed are those that conform sufficiently to the recognized standard for their type to be included in breeding programs and to be exhibited in competitions.

Sire — In a breeding pair of cats, the male is referred to as the sire.

Spay — Spaying is the surgical procedure whereby a female cat's ovaries are removed, rendering her incapable of reproduction.

Spray — Spraying is a territorial behavior typically seen in male cats. Using a stream of pungent urine, the cat marks its territory, often as part of a competition with other males for the attention of a female.

Stud — Studs are male cats that are intact and are therefore qualified to participate in a breeding program.

Subcutaneous — Subcutaneous means just below the skin, and typically refers to an injection or to the administration of supplemental fluids in cats with kidney deficiencies.

T

Tapetum Lucidum — The tapetum lucidum is the interior portion of a cat's eye. The structure is highly reflective and helps the cat to see effectively in low light. Cats cannot, however, see in total darkness.

V

Vaccine — Vaccines are dead or weakened preparations of a bacterium, virus, or other pathogen. They are injected into an individual for the purpose of stimulating the production of antibodies to cultivate immunity against disease.

W

Wean — Weaning is the point in a kitten's development when it gradually gives up its mother's milk as its primary means of nutrition and begins to take solid foods.

Whisker Break — The whisker break on a cat is an indentation on the upper jaw.

Whisker Pad — The whisker pads on a cat are the thickened areas on either side of the face that hold rows of sensory whiskers.

Whole — A cat of either gender that is intact, and has not been neutered or spayed.

Chocolate Tabby Persian
Photo Credit: Shannon McGraw of Meow House

Index

Lightning Source UK Ltd.
Milton Keynes UK
UKOW06f0858111017

310795UK00012B/716/P